The Complete Book of
SCRABBLE

The Complete Book of
SCRABBLE

GYLES BRANDRETH
Founder and Organiser of the
National Scrabble Championships

ROBERT HALE · LONDON

© Gyles Brandreth 1980
First published in Great Britain 1980
Reprinted 1981
Reprinted 1981

ISBN 0 7091 8385 2

SCRABBLE ® is the Registered Trade Mark owned in the United States of
America and in Canada by Selchow and Righter Co., New York, in Australia by
Scrabble Australia Pty Ltd., and in most other countries by members of the
J. W. Spear & Sons Ltd., Enfield, Greater London Group

Robert Hale Limited
Clerkenwell House
Clerkenwell Green
London, EC1

Photoset by
Specialised Offset Services Ltd., Liverpool
Printed in Great Britain by
Lowe & Brydone Ltd., Leeds, Yorkshire
and bound by Hunter & Foulis

Contents

Foreword

I was in Bristol Prison in the Spring of 1971 when I decided to launch the British National Scrabble Championships.

I wasn't an inmate you understand. I was just visiting – doing research for a book about prisons that I was then writing – and I happened to notice a couple of the prisoners playing my favourite game. I already knew that Scrabble was my family's favourite board game and the Royal Family's favourite board game, but I hadn't realised before that its popularity was so universal: that it could delight not just Her Majesty, but even those detained in her prisons at her pleasure. There and then I decided that any game that had such a breadth of appeal had to have its own national tournament.

Within a few days of my visit to Bristol, I inserted an advertisement in the Personal Column of *The Times* announcing the first ever National Scrabble Championships. I received three thousand replies – and they came from all sorts, from aristocrats and dustbin men (yes, really), from seven-year-olds and from octogenarians, from out-of-work actors and from overworked teachers – and I realised immediately that the competition was here to stay.

From its modest conception in Bristol Prison, the NSC has grown into quite a high-powered affair. We now get over 20,000 participants – and there are as many again who enquire about the competition but decide that they're not yet good enough to take part – and we run regional heats throughout the country as well as having a gruelling Grand Final. And because of the popularity of the competition and the fact that I have been its organiser for a decade now, Scrabble enthusiasts tend to look upon me as something of an authority on the game. I suppose they are right to do so, because over the years I must have witnessed more Scrabble games than I care to remember and I have observed and marvelled at the skill of the very best – and a few of the very worst – Scrabble players in the world.

In writing this book, I have attempted to create as complete a guide to the game as possible and I hope it will prove of value both to the novice and to the aspiring champion. One feature that certainly makes it unique among books on the subject is that the word lists printed here are based on *Chambers Twentieth Century Dictionary*, which only became the NSC 'word bible' in 1980. For the first nine years of the competition, the *Shorter Oxford English Dictionary* was the ultimate authority for the Championships, but we decided on a change to mark our tenth anniversary, and I am particularly grateful to Mrs Betty Kirkpatrick, Editor of *Chambers Dictionary* and Official Adjudicator at the British National Scrabble Championships for her help.

I am grateful to many other Scrabble enthusiasts as well, not least to my parents who introduced me to the game exactly a quarter of a century ago and to the late Mr J.H. Badley, the founder of Bedales School where I was a pupil, who taught me many of the secrets of Scrabble success when he was over 100 and I was just thirteen. From my point of view, the real pleasure of being the Organiser of the National Scrabble Championships is that I meet so many delightful people, not only the participants, but particularly the other organisers. The hard work involved in organising the Championships isn't done by me: it is done by Leonard and Cynthia Hodge, and by George Hanna and his remarkable team from J.W. Spear & Sons Ltd, the manufacturers of Scrabble. To all of them, and especially to Mr Francis Spear, the company's managing director (who was also a pupil at Bedales), and to his father, Mr Richard Spear, who originally gave me permission to write this book, my debt is obvious and immense.

Of all the labels that have been attached to me since I became involved in Scrabble – 'Scrabble King,' 'Scrabble Guru,' 'Mr

Scrabble,' 'Britain's Chief Scrabbler' – the one I treasure most appeared in a national newspaper noted for its inspired misprints. "Mr Gyles Brandreth," it said, "is the founder and organiser of the National Rabble Championships."

Let me say at once that there are no more civilised people on the planet than Scrabble players, but it can't be denied that passions *do* get roused in the run-up to the Finals of the NSC each June. As the poet – in this case, demented Scrabbler Robin Anderson – puts it so perfectly in his Ode to Scrabble:

> Where double beats treble but triple beats all
> But you may have to settle for nothing at all
> And chuck in your letters
> And grope for their betters
> And bring out a handful still worse than before;
> Where your noun if deemed proper
> Will bring you a cropper
> And a cheat is worth more than playing fair
> Where with just one E more
> You've a staggering score
> And your word may be rude – you don't care:
> You are plotting and scheming, quixotically dreaming
> Of clearing your tray and going out
> But the next player's eyed
> The place you had espied
> And your staggering score's up the spout;
> So you spring from your chair
> Raise the board in the air
> And smash it down hard round his ears –
> Other players are crying
> The letters are flying:
> You're charged and end up with three years.
> If your nerves are not icy, your temper is dicey,
> When losing, you tear out your hair –
> If you can't keep your cool
> Then follow the rule –
> When you dabble with Scrabble, beware!

1
The Scrabble Story

An Introduction to the History and Origins of the Game

Scrabble was not invented overnight, nor was it invented by just one person. The game was developed over a fifteen-year period, from 1933 to 1947, mainly by two Americans, Alfred Butts and James (Jim) Brunot, but with considerable casual effort from family and friends.

Alfred Butts was an architect by training. By 1931, because of the Great Depression, he was out of work. He had always had an interest in games, especially word-oriented games. As a boy, he was keen on anagrams, cards, crosswords, and cryptograms. By 1933, he had developed an ill-defined idea for a game called Lexiko. Butts had looked at all the existing games and analysed them. He found a surfeit of dice games, card games, board games with men, board games with counters, bingo, and so on. Butts decided that what was needed was a game using words, and with his background and interests, he felt that Lexiko could be developed into a marketable game, from which he could expect to make some money.

In the earliest version of Lexiko, there were letters and racks, but there was no board. Nor even was there the concept of a point value for each letter. Butts had analysed a large amount of newspaper text to determine the letter frequencies that he wanted for his 100 titles. At this early stage, the idea of the game was to try and make a seven-letter word with the letters in one's rack. If a word couldn't be made, unwanted letters were returned to the pool of unused ones, and some replacement letters were taken. The first

9

player to make a seven-letter word was the winner of that hand. Very simple, very straightforward.

The next stage in the development of Lexiko was the introduction of point values for the letters. Once a player had gone out with a seven-letter word, the other players were given the opportunity to play words of four, five or six letters. Scores were calculated for the words played, and, in this way, a ranking could be obtained for the players. Butts' friends liked the game, so he decided to send it to various games manufacturers. However, none was interested. All of them returned his game. None of them had any suggestions for improvements. Back to the drawing-board!

The next step in the game's development was the introduction of the board. Butts devised a board, introduced the idea of premium squares, and came up with the idea that words should be played in an interlocking fashion, like a crossword. The game now had its name changed. It was called, simply, It. Butts resubmitted the game to the major games manufacturers, but it was again rejected by all of them. Their reasons for rejection were that it was too serious, too complicated, too highbrow, too slow, not pictorially interesting, and not glamorous enough. Interestingly, at this stage, the game was also rejected by Selchow and Righter, the company which eventually produced and marketed Scrabble in the USA.

Butts' development of the game continued from 1933 to 1938, but every attempt to get it marketed led to nothing but rejections. In 1939, though, Butts was introduced to James (Jim) Brunot by a woman called Neva Deardorff. Brunot was a high-powered Government social work administrator, and Deardorff was a social worker. Deardorff already knew of Butts' game, and was something of a fanatic. She felt that Brunot might be interested in developing the game further and marketing it. Anyway, Butts introduced Brunot to his game, which by this time was called Criss-Crosswords. With the intervention of World War II, little effort was expended in trying to market the game. One abortive attempt was made in 1942 by a man called Chester Ives. Butts made up the game sets himself, and Ives was to market them from his bookshop in a town called Danbury, in Connecticut. For various reasons,

Ives took over the manufacture of the boards, but ran into problems. The exercise was fairly quickly abandoned, and yet one more attempt to get the game off the ground came to nothing.

During and after the War, Brunot had been continuing to amuse himself with the Criss-Crosswords game. At Deardorff's urging, Brunot and his business partner, Lester Twitchell, contacted Butts again, still with a view to producing and marketing the game. This was in 1946 or 1947. Various discussions took place, and the outcome was that the game was resurrected, renamed, and plans made for launching the game. Logo-Loco was one name that was almost chosen, but Scrabble was the final choice. The game was eventually launched in 1949 by Brunot through his Production and Marketing Company in Connecticut.

In the first year of production, 1949, a total of 2250 sets were sold, and the company made a loss. The following year 1950, saw 4800 sets sold, but still the company made a loss. The third full year of production, 1951, saw 8500 sets sold, but still the game failed to make any money for the company. Sales in the first half of 1952 were sluggish, and the prospects for the remainder of the year were not bright. But then, in the summer of 1952, the game took off with incredible success. Demand for the game was amazing. By 1954, Brunot's company had manufactured and sold $4\frac{1}{2}$ million sets of Scrabble. The USA was deep into a Scrabble craze. All the major magazines (*Look, Life*, and *Reader's Digest*) were running pieces about the game, and cartoons were appearing in newspapers and news-magazines.

So, what happened in the summer of 1952 that caused the game to take off the way that it did? New York City has a very large department store called Macy's. The chairman of Macy's board, Jack Strauss, had played the game in the summer of 1952 while on holiday with some friends. On returning to New York City, Strauss was amazed to find that Macy's didn't stock the game. This led to a big order from Macy's for the game. Macy's put a lot of effort into promoting it, and it took off from there.

Soon after its boom period started in 1952, Brunot's Production and Marketing Company came to an agreement with Selchow and

Righter about the manufacture and marketing of Scrabble. The arrangement was that Brunot's company would retain the rights to manufacture and market anything but the standard Scrabble set. Selchow and Righter would handle the standard set, and the Production and Marketing Company would still be able to make *de luxe* sets, foreign language sets, and so on.

The game then began to spread worldwide. It was introduced to Great Britain in 1954 by J.W. Spear and Sons Limited, who have successfully marketed it ever since. The game was introduced to Australia (the other great Scrabble stronghold after Great Britain and the USA) in 1953. The rights to market it there had been acquired by a Hungarian emigrant called Tibor Urban. Urban and his company, T.R. Urban, did much to put Scrabble on the map in Australia in the 1950s.

In 1971, Brunot sold outright all trademarks, copyrights and claims for his Scrabble game in the USA to Selchow and Righter, with payments to be made over five years, finishing in 1976. At the same time, Brunot sold the complete Australian rights to T.R. Urban and Company. The British and other rights were sold outright to J.W. Spear and Sons Limited.

That, briefly, is the story of Scrabble's development. Alfred Butts was the originator of the game, Jim Brunot provided the moving force in producing and marketing it, and Jack Strauss, the chairman of Macy's, was the catalyst who helped the game take off. Neva Deardorff brought Butts and Brunot together. And various friends and relatives of both Butts and Brunot contributed to the game's development with a host of suggestions for the various prototype versions of the game which ended up as Scrabble.

2
The Game of Scrabble

The rules of the game and how you play it. The rules interpreted and explained. The different regulations that apply in tournament Scrabble.

The Equipment

The basic equipment in any set of Scrabble consists of a board, 100 letter tiles, four racks, and a bag. The bag is for keeping the letter tiles in when a game is not in progress, and is also for keeping unused letter tiles in while a game is in progress. The racks are for players to keep their letter tiles on during the course of a game. The board measures 15 squares by 15 squares, and squares are of five different types, coloured grey, light blue, dark blue, pink and red. The grey squares are the 'non-premium' squares, and the other coloured ones are the 'premium' squares. Precisely how the different squares are to be used during the game is explained later.

The numbers of the different types of square are as follows:

> 164 grey squares
> 24 light blue squares
> 12 dark blue squares
> 17 pink squares
> 8 red squares

The light blue squares are called the double-letter-score squares; the dark blue squares are called the triple-letter-score squares; the pink squares are called the double-word-score squares; and the red squares are called the triple-word-score squares. Figure 1 shows the

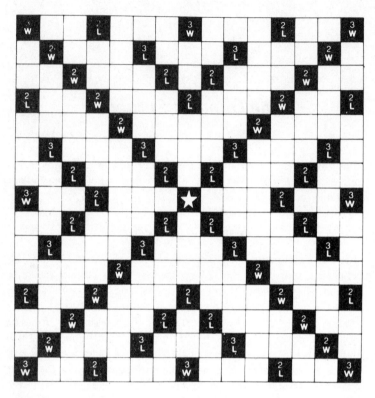

Figure 1

layout of the squares on a standard board. The double-letter-score squares are marked 2L; the triple-letter-score squares are marked 3L; the double-word-score squares are marked 2W; and the triple-word-score squares are marked 3W. The board's centre square, marked in Figure 1 with a white star, is also a double-word-score square. It is distinctively marked because the rules of the game stipulate that the first word played on the board must cover this square. The 100 letter tiles are made up of two blank tiles and 98 tiles bearing letters and associated point values. The number of different letters and their corresponding point values are as follows:

letter	number in a set	point value
A	9	1
B	2	3
C	2	3
D	4	2
E	12	1
F	2	4
G	3	2
H	2	4
I	9	1
J	1	8
K	1	5
L	4	1
M	2	3
N	6	1
O	8	1
P	2	3
Q	1	10
R	6	1
S	4	1
T	6	1
U	4	1
V	2	4
W	2	4
X	1	8
Y	2	4
Z	1	10
blank	2	0

Variations in Equipment

De luxe versions of the board are available. These have ridges on all four sides of each square on the board. These stop letter tiles from slipping about on the board as it is moved. To further ease the movement of the board, it is constructed underneath with a circular ridge, so that it can revolve quite easily.

Travel versions of the game also exist. In a travel set, the board is only about one quarter the size of a board in a standard or de luxe version of the set. On the travel version of the board, there are holes at the four corners of the squares. All of the letter tiles have four pegs on their lower sides, and these pegs fit into the holes on the board. This allows the tiles to be firmly pressed into position on the board, and the board can be moved about quite freely without the tiles falling off.

Outline of the Game

Scrabble is a word game that can be played by two, three or four players. Played seriously, it is essentially a game for two players. The game consists of players forming interlocking words on the board, using the letter tiles. All words are to be connected, as in an ordinary crossword puzzle. Players score points for the words which they make. Scores are calculated depending on the point values of the tiles played and also the types of squares on the board which the letters have been placed on. Play passes from player to player until all of the tiles are exhausted, and one player has no more tiles left on his rack. The winner of the game is the player who has scored the highest total number of points during the course of the game. The remainder of this book describes the rules governing where and how words can be placed on the board, how to calculate scores, and how to get the highest scores possible.

Rules for Playing

To begin with, all the tiles should be placed in the bag provided with the game and they should be given a thorough shaking. (Bags are only provided with the travel and *de luxe* editions of the game. If you own a standard set, you will have to make your own bag.) Alternatively, the tiles may be placed face down in the upturned lid of the box which the game came in, and then they should be thoroughly shuffled. From now on, the tiles in the bag or the lid will be referred to as 'the pool of unused letters' or just 'the pool'. Each player now chooses one tile from the pool. The player with the letter nearest to the beginning of the alphabet has the first move. If two or more players choose the same letter and no other player has a letter nearer to the beginning of the alphabet, the players should return their letters to the pool and draw replacement letters. Once the first player has been chosen in this way, the subsequent order of play is clockwise round the board. However, if players want to choose some alternative method for selecting the first player and the subsequent order of play, they may do so, but all players must be agreed about the method beforehand.

Once the order of play has been determined, all letters are returned to the pool and are well mixed. The first player then chooses seven tiles without looking at them, and places them on his rack. Other players then take it in turn to select seven letters, each of them making sure that none of the other players can see his letters.

The First Play

Whichever player was chosen to go first uses two or more of his letters to form a word on the board. The word may be placed horizontally or vertically, such that one of its letters covers the centre square on the board. Words may never be played diagonally. A player completes his turn by counting his score and announcing it to the other players. Scoring is described in detail a

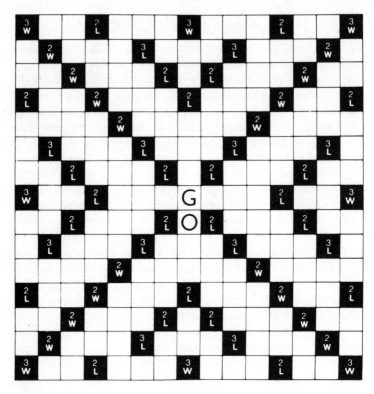

Figure 2

little later on. The score made by the player is recorded by one of the players who was chosen to keep a note of the scores at the beginning of the game. After announcing his score, the first player then takes as many tiles from the pool of unused letters as he has just played on the board, ending up with seven tiles on his rack again. Figures 2 and 3 show possible boards after the first move in each of two games.

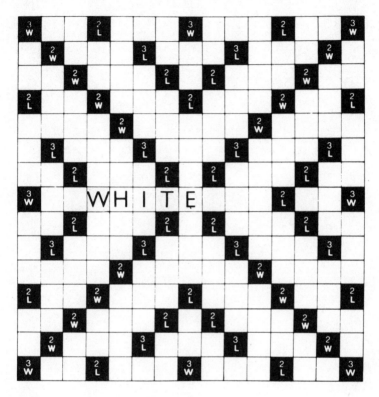

Figure 3

The Subsequent Plays

After the very first move, players take it in turn to add one or more tiles to those already on the board, forming one or more new words at each turn. Tiles may only be placed horizontally or vertically adjacent to a tile already on the board or one just played on the board. If the letters played touch other letters in neighbouring rows or columns, they must also form complete words. Each player gets full credit not only for the new words he puts down, but also for

Figure 4

modifying words that may already have been on the board. The score for a turn is the sum of the scores for each of the words made or modified by the player at his turn. Words can be formed in three different ways, all or any of which could be put into effect at one particular turn. The three ways are described here.

1. A word can be formed by adding one or more letters to a word which is already on the board, turning it into a new different word. Examples are shown in Figures 4-8. In each of them, the word GO was already on the board. In Figure 4, the single letter T has

Figure 5

been added to the end of GO, forming the new word GOT. In Figure 5, the single letter E has been added at the beginning of GO, forming the new word EGO. In Figure 6, three letters, ING, have been added to the end of GO, to form the new word GOING. In Figure 7, two letters, SA, have been added at the beginning of GO, to form the new word SAGO. And in Figure 8, letters have been added to the beginning and end of GO, forming the new word AGONY.

21

Figure 6

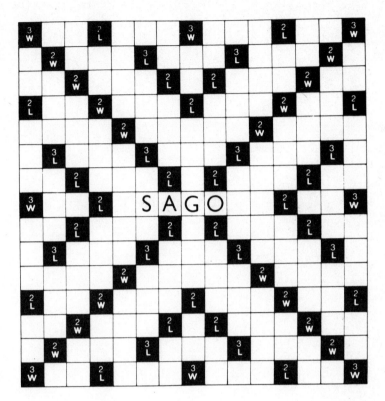

Figure 7

Figure 8

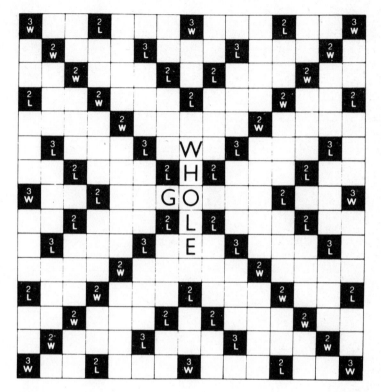

Figure 9

2. A word can be formed by playing a word perpendicularly to a word already on the board. The new word must either use one of the letters of the word already on the board, or must add a letter to the word already on the board, making a second new word in the process. Examples are shown in Figures 9 and 10. In Figure 9, the word GO was already on the board. Four letters, WH and LE, are added to the O of GO, forming the new word WHOLE. As WHOLE is the only new word made, it is the only word for which points can be scored. In Figure 10, the word GO was already on the board.

Figure 10

The vertical word EATEN is now placed on the board, turning GO into GOT at the same time. Two new words have been formed, EATEN and GOT, and points are to be scored for both of them. The total score for the move is the sum of the scores for each of the individual new words formed.

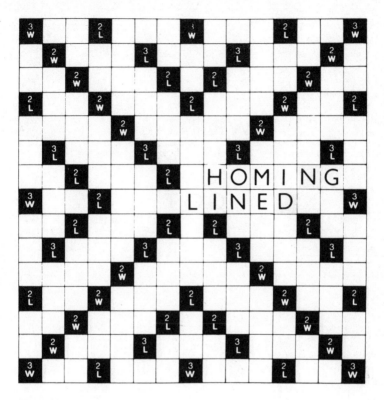

Figure 11

3. A word can be played parallel to a word already on the board, so that adjoining letters form new words. Figure 11 gives an example of this. The word LINED was already on the board. The new word HOMING is then played parallel to it, forming the new words HI, ON, ME and ID at the same time. All five of these new words score points. The total score for the move is the sum of the points scored by each of the words separately.

In all cases, after the first word has been played, across the centre square of the board, all other words played must interlock

Figure 12

with other words already on the board. No word or words can be in isolation from the other words on the board.

As well as forming words in the three ways described above, it is possible to form words which are essentially different combinations of the three methods. Examples are given in Figures 12-14. In Figure 12, the words GO, RING, WRITE and TO are already on the board. The letters TTER are added to the end of TO, forming TOTTER, and also turning GO into GOT at the same time. In Figure 13, the words ATONE, AM, ME, GATE, SIN and STOP

Figure 13

are already on the board. Using the A of GATE and the I of SIN, the horizontal word RATION is formed. At the same time, the vertical words RAM, TO, TOE and ON are also formed. In Figure 14, the words GOAT and RAG are already on the board. The horizontal word MENTOR is played, turning RAG into RAGE, and forming the new words ON, AT and TO.

Figure 14

Exchanging Tiles

At his turn, a player may decide not to place any tiles on the board, or, indeed, may be totally unable to place any tiles at all on the board. In this case, any or all of the tiles on his rack may be exchanged for an equivalent number of tiles from the pool of unused letters. The unwanted tiles must first be removed from his rack, new ones are selected from the pool, the unwanted ones returned to the pool and the pool then thoroughly mixed. A player must decide on which tiles he wants to get rid of before taking new ones from the pool. A player cannot change tiles and place tiles on the board at the same time. He can do one or other, but not both. Towards the end of the game when there are only a few tiles left in the pool of unused ones, a player cannot exchange more tiles than there actually are in the pool. If the pool only has four tiles in it and a player wants to exchange five tiles, he can't. He can exchange up to four tiles only, or decide to actually place some tiles on the board instead.

If a player wants to exchange his tiles at the very first move of the game, he is entitled to do so. The second player, who then becomes the first player to actually place a word on the board, must observe the same requirements as he would if he was the first player. Namely, he must play at least two tiles, and the word must cover the centre square of the board.

The official Scrabble rules do not impose any limit on the number of exchanges that a player may make during the course of a game. However, some players do impose such a rule. In any game where there is such a limit, all players should be clear from the outset as to exactly how many exchanges will be allowed.

The reasons why a player might prefer to exchange some or all of his tiles will be looked at in more detail later on.

Missing a Turn

A player is not allowed to miss a turn, unless he cannot make a word and there are no tiles remaining in the pool. He *must* either place one or more tiles on the board or exchange one or more tiles. However, some players are not particularly fussy about enforcing this rule, allowing players to pass as they wish. As will be seen later, though, there is usually little point in just passing.

Blank Tiles

The two blank tiles in the set of 100 tiles have no point value. They are each worth nothing. And yet, they are the most valuable tiles in the whole set. Just why this is so will become apparent later. A blank tile may be used to represent any letter that its player wishes. When a player puts a word on the board which uses a blank, he must state what letter the blank represents. Thereafter, the blank continues to represent that letter until the end of the game. The letter represented by a blank cannot be changed part way through a game. In the standard version of Scrabble, once a blank has been played on the board, it cannot be removed from the board. (There is a variant version of the game which allows blanks to be removed from the board, as long as they are replaced by the letters which they are representing. The blanks may then be used to represent other letters when they are subsequently played.)

Scoring

A list of the point values of the different letters was given earlier. In general, the commoner letters are worth 1-2 points, the uncommon letters are worth 8-10 points, and the other letters fall between these extremes, being worth 3-5 points. The premium (coloured) squares and the non-premium (grey) squares have already been described. Now is the time to see how the point values and squares are used in calculating the score for a move made by a player. The five different types of square (grey, light blue, dark blue, pink, and red) all affect the scores of the words played on the squares. The effects of the differently coloured squares are now described.

1. If a letter of a word is placed on a grey square, the letter scores the point value shown on the face of the tile. (In the figures in this book, grey squares are shown as white squares.)

2. If a letter of a word is placed on a double-letter-score square, the letter scores *twice* the point value shown on the face of the tile.

3. If a letter of a word is placed on a triple-letter-score square, the letter scores *three times* the point value shown on the face of the tile.

4. If a letter of a word is placed on a double-word-score square, the letter only scores the point value shown on the face of the tile, but *doubles* the total point value of the whole word. That is, all the individual letter point scores are doubled. This doubling only takes effect after the effects of the double-letter-score and triple-letter score squares have been taken into consideration.

5. If a letter of a word is placed on a triple-word-score square, the letter only scores the point value shown on the face of the tile, but *triples* the total point value of the whole word. That is, all the individual letter point scores are tripled. This tripling only takes effect after the effects of the double-letter-score and triple-letter-score squares have been taken into consideration.

Once a tile has been placed on a premium square, that square has *no* premium value for any subsequent moves, even though the word in which the square is used may be modified. Put another way, a premium square only has an effect for the first move in which it is used. Thereafter, it should just be treated as a grey (non-premium) square.

Figures 15 and 16 give examples of how premium squares are to be used in calculating a word's score. In Figure 15, the word GO is put down as the very first word on the board. The G scores 2 points (its face value), and the O scores 1 point (its face value). The two letters together score 3 points, but, since the G falls on a double-word-score square, the point value of the whole word is 3 points

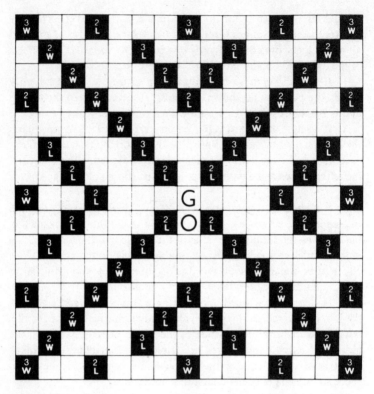

Figure 15

doubled, or 6 points. So the score for that particular move is 6 points. In Figure 16, the word WHITE is put down as the very first word on the board, the W falling on a double-letter-score square. The W is worth twice its face value because of this; that is, 8 points. The H, I and T all fall on grey squares, and so score only their face value numbers of points (respectively, 4 points, 1 point and 1 point). The E falls on a double-word-score square, and so has a

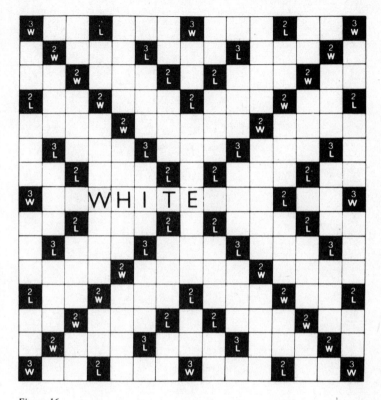

Figure 16

value of only 1 point, but causes the total point value of all the letters to be doubled. Thus:

$$W \quad H \quad I \quad T \quad E$$
$$8 + 4 + 1 + 1 + 1 = 15$$

Figure 17

But these 15 points have to be doubled, giving 30 points as the total score for the word. Figure 17 illustrates another example. The word LIVE was already on the board. Using the L of LIVE, six letters were then played to form the word CHILLED. None of the letters just played has covered a double-letter-score or triple-letter-score square. Accordingly, all the letters of CHILLED score points equal to their face values. Thus:

$$\text{C} \quad \text{H} \quad \text{I} \quad \text{L} \quad \text{L} \quad \text{E} \quad \text{D}$$
$$3 + 4 + 1 + 1 + 1 + 1 + 2 = 13$$

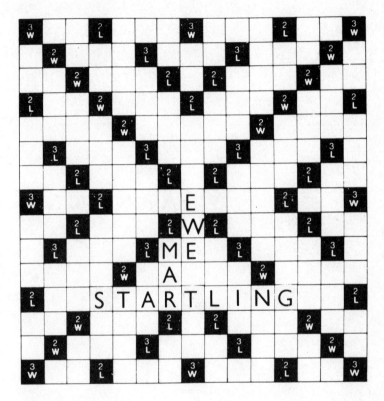

Figure 18

But since the word stretched across two double-word-score squares, the 13 points must be doubled twice; that is, quadrupled. So the word actually scores a total of 52 points. This should begin to demonstrate the power of the double-word-score squares. Figure 18 demonstrates yet another example. The words EWE, ME, MAR and TAR are already on the board. Using the word TAR, the new word STARTLING is formed. The second T falls on a double-letter-score square, and so is worth 2 points. The other letters all score points equal to their face values. Thus:

$$S \quad T \quad A \quad R \quad T \quad L \quad I \quad N \quad G$$
$$1 + 1 + 1 + 1 + 2 + 1 + 1 + 1 + 2 = 11$$

Figure 19

But as the word covers two double-word-score squares, the 11 points must be doubled twice; that is, quadrupled. So the total score for the word is 44 points. This should demonstrate the need to take into account the effects of double-letter-score (and triple-letter-score) squares before applying the effects of the double-word-score (and triple-word-score) squares. A further example is offered by Figure 19. The word EARN is already on the board. It is subsequently turned into YEARNINGS. The I falls on a double-letter-score square and the S falls on a triple-word-score square. The total score of the word is calculated thus:

$$
\begin{array}{ccccccccc}
\text{Y} & \text{E} & \text{A} & \text{R} & \text{N} & \text{I} & \text{N} & \text{G} & \text{S} \\
4 & + 1 & + 1 & + 1 & + 1 & + 2 & + 1 & + 2 & + 1 = 14
\end{array}
$$

But the 14 points must be tripled, because of the premium square covered by the S. So the total score for the word is 42 points.

So, to summarise: when a word is formed and it covers more than one premium square *at that move*, the total score for the word is calculated by working out the scores for all the letters individually, taking into account the effects of the double-letter-score and triple-letter-score squares, adding them together, and then doubling or tripling the score as necessary, depending on how many double-word-score and triple-word-score squares have also been covered *at that move*.

If a blank tile is placed on a double-letter-score or triple-letter-score square, it has no effect. Twice nothing is nothing, and three times nothing is nothing. But, if the blank tile falls on a double-word-score or triple-word-score square, the point value of the whole word is still doubled or tripled, as necessary, even though the blank itself contributes no points at all.

If two or more words are formed at the same turn, they are all scored, as described above, and the total score for the turn is the sum of the scores for all of the words made. Common letters are counted, with their full premium values, if any, in the score for each of the words in which they occur. Figure 20 offers an example. The words NICE and AN are already on the board. The word ACHE is now played horizontally, turning AN into CAN at the same time. Because the C falls on a triple-letter-score square, it contributes 9 points to both ACHE and CAN. Thus:

$$A \quad C \quad H \quad E$$
$$1 + 9 + 4 + 1 = 15$$

and

$$C \quad A \quad N$$
$$9 + 1 + 1 = 11$$

The 15 points and the 11 points have to be added together to get the total score for the move. The total is, of course, 26 points.

Figure 20

Figure 21

A powerful example of the cumulative effect of premium squares is given in Figure 21. The words FRO, CHAR, HALF, OFTEN, ON and ONE are already on the board. Playing the single letter Z just to the left of ONE causes two new words to be formed, ZONE and FROZE. Because the Z occurs in both words, it contributes its tripled score (because it is on a triple-letter-score square) to both of the words. Thus:

$$Z \quad O \quad N \quad E$$
$$30 + 1 + 1 + 1 = 33$$

and

$$F \quad R \quad O \quad Z \quad E$$
$$4 + 1 + 1 + 30 + 1 = 37$$

Figure 22

The 33 points and the 37 points have to be added together to get the total score for the move. The total is, of course, 70 points. Just for playing one letter!

Once the basic method of scoring is mastered, even the most complicated of cases should offer no problems. Consider the example shown in Figure 22. The words HORN, MOON, MOUNT, TANGO, TAP, ON and TIN are already on the board. By playing the letters SIGH in front of the T of TIN, and the letter G after TIN, the horizontal word SIGHTING and the vertical

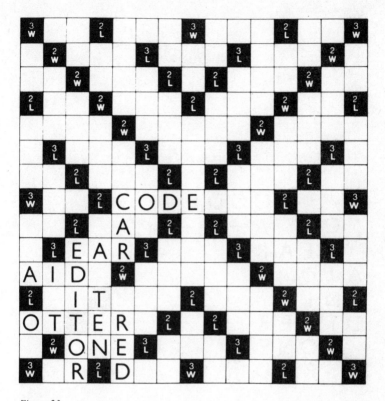

Figure 23

words TAPS and OH are formed. The total score is calculated by
first working out the score for each of the words separately. Thus:

$$T \quad A \quad P \quad S$$
$$1 + 1 + 3 + 1 = 6$$

But this has to be tripled as the S falls on a triple-word-score
square. So, the total for TAPS is 18 points. The score for OH is
worked out like this:

$$O \quad H$$
$$1 + 8 = 9$$

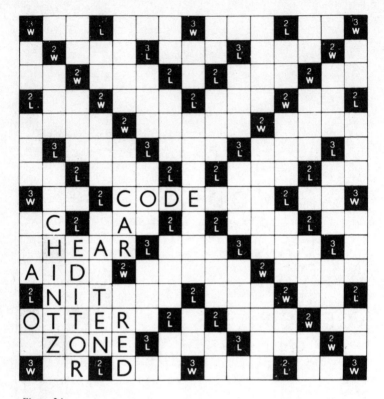

Figure 24

And SIGHTING:

$$\begin{array}{cccccccc} S & I & G & H & T & I & N & G \\ 1 + & 1 + & 2 + & 8 + & 1 + & 1 + & 1 + & 2 = 17 \end{array}$$

But as the S and final G have both just been placed on triple-word-score squares, the 17 points have to be tripled, and tripled again, giving 153 points. The total score for the move is got by adding together the scores for the three words separately (18 points, 9 points, and 153 points), giving a total score of 180 points!

Another complicated example is shown in Figure 23. The words CODE, CAR, EAR, EDITOR, AID, OTTER, EN, RED and ONE are all already on the board. The four letters C, H, N and Z are added, as shown in Figure 24. This has resulted in the four words CHINTZ, HEAR, NIT and ZONE being formed. You should be able to work out that CHINTZ scores 56 points, HEAR scores 15 points, NIT scores 3 points, and ZONE scores 26 points; giving a total score of exactly 100 points. Using a high-value letter in two words and doubling the score for each word, as the Z has done here, usually brings in a considerable score. So much the better, too, if you can incorporate a double-letter-score or triple-letter-score square with a high-value letter (like the H here).

The 50-point Bonus

If a player uses all seven of his tiles at a single turn, not only does he get the score for that move, worked out as described above, but he also gets a bonus of 50 points as well. The 50-point bonus must be added after the effects of any premium squares have been taken into account. Obviously using up one's tiles in one go and getting a 50-point bonus can boost a player's score quite dramatically, especially if this can be done several times in a game. The importance of achieving such bonuses must be emphasised. Later parts of this book will tell you how to aim for such bonuses, working for them rather than just waiting for them to happen by chance. By chance, they happen very infrequently; by design, they can be made to happen a good deal more often.

Figure 25

Figure 25 offers an example of a move which uses up all seven of a player's letters at one turn. The word REVOKES is played with the R falling on the centre square and the K falling on the double-letter-score square. The score for the word is 19 points, doubled, plus the 50-point bonus, giving a total score of 88 points for the move. Note the importance of ensuring that the highest value letter falls on the double-letter-score square. If REVOKES had

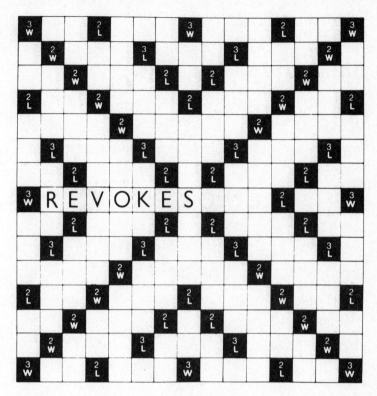

Figure 26

been played as in Figure 26, with the V on the double-letter-score square on the opposite side of the board, then it would only have scored 86 points. If the player had placed the word such that any of the letters other than K or V fell on the double-letter-score square, as in Figure 27, the total score would have been only 80 points.

Figure 27

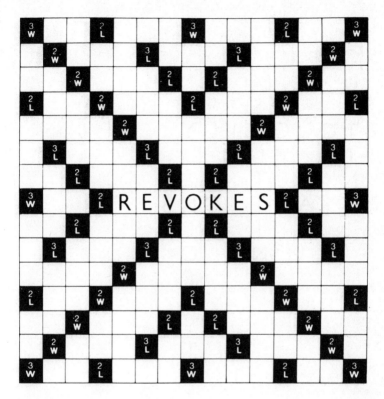

Figure 28

Even less desirable, the player might have played the word so that none of the letters fell on the double-letter-score square, as in Figure 28. This scores 78 points. Even when playing words which involve 50-point bonuses, you should not be oblivious to maximising the scores achieved for the letters in the words. This simple example offered here demonstrates a 10-point difference between the best and worst places for the word REVOKES played at the first turn of a game. The same principle should be borne in mind, of course, even when you are not playing for bonuses.

49

Figure 29

To ensure that you fully understand the scoring when 50-point bonuses are involved, Figure 29 offers five examples of bonus words. The first player puts down the word ACTIONS. (The C is on a double-letter-score square and the whole word covers a double-word-score square). The total score for this is 74 points. The second player follows this with SHUTTING, scoring 98 points. (This covers two double-word-score squares, but no double-letter-score or triple-letter-score squares.) The third word played is NEOPHYTE, using the N of ACTIONS. This scores 110 points.

(Note that the H falls on a double-letter-score square and the word covers a triple-word-score square.) TOUCHILY is played as the fourth word. No premium squares at all are covered, so the word scores only 66 points. The fifth word played is DOUBTING, using the T of TOUCHILY. (The B falls on a double-letter-score square and the word covers two triple-word-score squares.) The total score for the word is 185 points! Of course, in real-life games, successions of 50-point bonuses do not happen particularly often. Even the most expert of players would be pleased with three or four bonuses during the course of one game.

Scoring at the End of the Game

A game comes to an end when *either* one player has used all of his tiles and there are none left in the pool *or* none of the players is able to make a move and there are no tiles left in the pool. At the close of a game, each player's total score up to that stage is reduced by the points value of the unplayed tiles left on his rack. If one of the players has used all of his tiles, his score is increased by the sum of the unplayed tiles on the racks of all of his opponents. Here is an example from a game involving four players. Suppose that just before the last move the scores of the four players were as follows:

player 1	155 points
player 2	195 points
player 3	215 points
player 4	170 points

Player 1 uses all the letters left on his rack, leaving none in the pool. Say he scores 10 points with his last move, bringing his score up to 165 points. Assume that his opponents are left with the letters shown:

player 2	AAEEO
player 3	QVX
player 4	M blank

The value of player 2's letters is 5 points, so his score goes down to 190 points; the value of player 3's letters is 22 points, so his score goes down to 193 points; and the value of player 4's letters is 3 points, so his score goes down to 167 points. (Notice that player 4 does not get penalised at all for being caught with a blank tile.) Player 1's total score is increased by 5 points (from player 2), by another 22 points (from player 3), and by another 3 points (from player 4), giving him 195 points altogether. The final position is this:

player 1   195 points
player 2   190 points
player 3   193 points
player 4   167 points

Notice how before he made his last move, player 1 was lying fourth. But by going out and catching his opponents for all their letters, he has leapfrogged over them all, and wins the game!

Keeping Track of the Scores

At the beginning of a game, one person should be chosen to record the scores. Precisely how this score-keeper is to be chosen can be left to the players concerned. The score-keeper should draw up a sheet headed with each player's name. Beneath each name should be two columns, one to record the points scored at each move, and the other to record that player's running total score. Suppose that players 1, 2 and 3 successively score 20, 15, 8, 65, 9, 25, 18, 30, 72, 8, 0 and 42 points (the score of 0 points indicating a change of tiles), the score sheet should then look something like this:

player 1		player 2		player 3	
20	20	15	15	8	8
65	85	9	24	25	33
18	103	30	54	72	105
8	111	0	54	42	147

You should keep a running total as well as the individual move totals. This enables all the players to ensure that all of their scores have been recorded and to see how they are doing relative to the other players at any stage in the game. Even if a player exchanges some of his tiles, keep track of this, too. In this way, all the columns should be of the same length at the end of each round, and it will be immediately apparent that someone's score has been omitted if the columns do not line up. Occasionally, players might want to reconstruct the exact course of a game. Having a record of the scores at every stage certainly helps this to be done.

Words

Up until now nothing has been said about the acceptability or otherwise of words which are played. What happens if a player spells a word incorrectly? Or if one player puts down a word which an opponent hasn't heard of? The official rules of the game state that any words found in a standard dictionary are permitted, with the exception of those beginning with a capital letter, those marked as being foreign, and those being spelt with an apostrophe or a hyphen. Abbreviations are not allowed, either. Because dictionaries can differ so much, it is wise for players to agree on a dictionary of authority at the start of a game. Some dictionaries contain only a few tens of thousands of words; others contain well over half a million. Dictionaries are published at different dates; today's neologism may well not be in a dictionary published over a decade ago. Also, dictionaries have different attitudes to certain classes of words. For example, obsolete words are treated extensively in some dictionaries, and completely omitted from others; other dictionaries treat Scots words extensively, while some include only a handful; technical words get short shrift in certain dictionaries, but are treated much more fully in other dictionaries. So, choose a dictionary that all players agree on before the game actually gets under way.

If a player is not sure about a word played by an opponent, the rules give him the right to challenge it. The word is then looked up in the agreed dictionary, preferably by both the players concerned. If the word is in the dictionary and does not contravene any of the official rules, the word is allowed, and remains on the board. If the word is not allowable, the letter tiles which have just been played should be removed from the board and returned to the rack of the player from which they came. This player loses his turn, and play passes to the next player. After a word has been played, the player should allow a reasonable amount of time to pass, to ensure that there are no challenges. If he selects some new tiles from the pool, and then the word he has just played is challenged and found unacceptable, there may be disputes about which tiles should be put back into the pool. Further, it saves having to alter the entries on the score sheet.

If a player challenges a word and it is found to be allowable, there is no penalty imposed on the challenger. He does not lose his next turn, nor does he forfeit any points. Some players feel that unsuccessful challenges should lead to some form of penalty being imposed. If players want to introduce such a 'house rule' for their own games, it must be clearly understood and agreed to by all players at the start of the game. To reiterate, though, the official Scrabble rules do not penalise an unsuccessful challenger. This is probably quite wise, for players would be more inclined to try words that they were not quite sure about, in the hope that their opponents will not challenge for fear of incurring a penalty. Such a situation would be undesirable.

A word may only be challenged immediately after the turn at which it has been made and before the next turn. A challenge made after some intervening move is not allowed, even if the word challenged is obviously invalid. This is sensible as it saves problems about players returning tiles to the pool, picking up tiles which have been played on the board in the interim, and adjusting the score sheet. Players should make sure that they are happy with all words played before the next move is made.

Most dictionaries include obsolete words, archaic words, dialect words and slang words, though to different extents. The official rules do not bar any of these, but some players are unhappy about using such words, particularly obsolete ones. Again, there can be no objection to a 'house rule' forbidding the use of certain categories of words, as long as all players understand and agree to the rule before play starts.

Dictionaries

Dictionaries have been mentioned in passing in the preceding section, but they will be looked at in a little more detail now. The official Scrabble rules allow for the use of any standard dictionary. Here are some dictionaries used by Scrabble players, with some relevant comments about each.

Chambers Twentieth Century Dictionary (with 1977 Supplement): this has about 250,000 words, including many neologisms that have entered the English language in the past decade or two. Foreign words are clearly marked as being such; obsolete words are usually marked as being so, though there is a smattering of words, all probably obsolete, which are just described as 'old spellings'; abbreviations are distinguishable by the use of the word 'abbreviation', though the distinction between these and contractions and shortened forms is not clear. Words that are usually spelled with an initial capital letter are clearly shown by the dictionary as having the capital; words usually requiring a lower-case initial letter are shown as having the lower-case letter.

The Concise Oxford Dictionary (6th edition, 1976): this contains about 74,000 items, so is considerably smaller than Chambers. There are few if any obsolete words. No words appear to be marked as foreign, and all abbreviations are quite clearly marked. Only those words that are usually spelled with an initial capital letter actually have one in the dictionary.

The Shorter Oxford English Dictionary (3rd edition, 1944, but with numerous reprintings and different supplement sections): this contains around 200,000 words, a large number of them being obsolete, archaic and foreign. Foreign words are clearly distinguished, though not all players will be happy to accept the dictionary's ruling here. Both IGLOO and VODKA are marked as foreign still, even though they can be said to have entered the English language quite some time ago. The biggest drawback to using this dictionary is that every single entry begins with a capital letter. Accordingly, if a word is being challenged on the suspicion that it might be a proper noun, this dictionary can offer no support one way or the other.

The Oxford English Dictionary (1933): this is a very large and very expensive dictionary. It contains a vast number of obsolete words and omits most of the words which have entered the language since the 1920s, as well as many that entered English towards the end of the nineteenth century. It suffers from the same problem as the *Shorter Oxford English Dictionary*; namely, it capitalises every entry. This is not a very practical dictionary for Scrabble players.

Webster's New Collegiate Dictionary (8th edition, 1973): this has approximately 150,000 entries, a large number of which are proper names (clearly shown to have initial capital letters) and multi-word phrases. As it is an American dictionary, many words are shown with their American spellings. For example, COLOR and VALOR are both shown, with COLOUR and VALOUR listed merely as British variant spellings. It contains very few if any obsolete words, but contains many neologisms which Chambers does not include.

Webster's Third New International Dictionary (1961): this is the American equivalent of the *Oxford English Dictionary*, but is a lot more up-to-date. It contains about 450,000 words. No words at all are marked as foreign; because all can be found in English text, the dictionary-makers have seen fit not to single out any of them as being foreign. It contains a large number of obsolete, dialect, and archaic words. It shows the plural form of every noun, all the forms of every verb, and the comparative and superlative forms of adjectives where these are commonly found. This is something that no other dictionary does on such an extensive scale, and is one of the big plusses of this dictionary. As far as proper nouns are concerned, it suffers from the inverse problem that the *Oxford*

English Dictionary and the *Shorter Oxford English Dictionary* suffer from. Namely, it lists all words, including proper nouns, with a lower-case initial letter. Then, using a series of labels (such as 'capitalised', 'usually capitalised', 'often capitalised' and 'sometimes capitalised'), it offers some idea of whether the word is spelled with or without an initial capital letter. This can all be somewhat confusing for the Scrabble player! Again, as it is an American dictionary, American spellings abound, though the British equivalents are invariably given.

American Scrabble enthusiasts can also acquire *The Official Scrabble Player's Dictionary*, which is used in tournaments throughout the U.S., but which is not valid in the U.K. and does not have a British equivalent.

The National Scrabble Championship

The National Scrabble Championship was first run in 1971, and has taken place every year since then. For the Championship and the preceding Regional games, there are only ever two players in a game. Three-player and four-player games are never played. As would be expected with any National Championship, whether it is hockey, chess or Scrabble, there are very well-defined rules. These rules are imposed in addition to the official rules which accompany every set of Scrabble. This section summarises the rules that apply to the National Scrabble Championship Finals from 1980 onwards.

Players have a maximum of two minutes per move. An adjudicator with a stop-clock is provided for every pair of players, and his responsibility is to let the players know when their time is nearly finished and completely finished. If a player does not make a move within the two minutes, he forfeits his turn.

Players are allowed to exchange their tiles for others in the pool no more than three times in a game.

Words

The rules governing the acceptability or otherwise of words are quite complicated, but have been worked out over the years by many experts, including dictionary-makers. Rules such as these will always be necessary for a National Championship or even games played on a local club basis. However, you may find the rules unnecessary for friendly, fireside games, preferring to judge each challenged word on its merits, or even to vote on it.

At the Finals of the National Scrabble Championships, all words must be in the latest edition of *Chambers Twentieth Century Dictionary*, either in the main body of the dictionary or in the supplement of new words. All the following rules about specific groups of words apply solely to this particular dictionary.

Words listed only with an initial capital letter are not allowed, unless there is something to indicate that the word can also be spelled with a lower-case initial letter. For example, PILSENER is shown with a capital P, but a note about it says 'also without capital'. The word BAYARD is shown only with a capital B, but for one of the definitions, the note 'without capital' is added. Accordingly, both PILSENER and BAYARD would be allowable.

Foreign words are not permitted. A foreign word is one which has a foreign language label, occurring in round brackets, immediately after the word's entry in the dictionary. For example, ABSIT is shown to be Latin by the presence of an L in round brackets. Examples of other foreign words include CADEAU (French), CIAO (Italian), and ALTEZA (Spanish). Other languages which are taken to be foreign include Afrikaans (e.g. MOOI), American (e.g. COLOR), Australian (e.g. POMMY), Indian (e.g. KUMARI), Irish (e.g. ASTHORE), New Zealand (e.g. KAI), South African (e.g. NEK), and Welsh (e.g. CWM). Words are permitted which are of foreign origin and have this indicated in some way in the etymology, which is given in square brackets at the end of each word's entry. For example, all the following are allowable; none is marked as foreign, even though their etymologies confirm their foreign appearance. EWIGKEIT,

KAKI, KALPIS, LIKIN, PANOCHA and QUA are all quite valid.

Words of which all meanings are marked as obsolete are not permitted. For example, NE and SWITH are both obsolete in all their meanings; but, PICKEER and REIGN, though they have some obsolete meanings, do have some which are not obsolete. Accordingly, PICKEER and REIGN are allowed. All words which are archaic are allowed, unless some other rule is contravened.

Words of which all meanings are marked as coming from the works of Shakespeare, Spenser and Milton are not permitted. For example, HOX (Shakespeare), YGO (Spenser) and SDEIGNE (Spenser and Milton) are not allowed. If a word is given a meaning that is marked as having been used by one of these three authors, it is not necessarily unallowable. If a meaning is given which is not obsolete, not from Shakespeare, Spenser, or Milton, then the word is allowable. Here are some examples of allowable words: QUAT (only one of its two meanings is given as Shakespearean), THEE (not all definitions are from Spenser), and RAVIN (though some meanings are marked as coming from all three authors, there are meanings which make the word allowable).

Words designated as abbreviations are not allowable; for example, COSEC and METHS. But, words designated as contractions and shortened forms are allowable; for example, COZ and MA are shown as contractions, and HYPE and KILO are shown as short forms.

Words which are defined as letters or letter sounds are not permitted, unless they have some other meaning. For example, AITCH and EF are not allowed, but EM and ZED are. (An EM is a unit of measurement used by printers, and a ZED is an iron bar in the shape of the letter Z). This same rule extends to letters from foreign languages. For example, VAU and XI are not allowed, but ALPHA and ZETA are. (An ALPHA is the brightest star of a constellation, and a ZETA is a small room or closet.)

Words requiring an apostrophe (e.g. DON'T and BO'S'N) or a hyphen (e.g. GO-KART and HI-FI) are not allowed.

Plurals of nouns formed by the addition of S or ES (e.g. HOPS and RICHES) will be allowed where these plurals are likely to exist in English, whether or not they are in the dictionary, unless some other plural form is specifically shown by the dictionary. For example, the dictionary actually shows these plural forms: OXEN, RADII and RADICES. The addition of ES to a singular noun may also be accompanied by a change of a final Y to an I; for example, CURRY to CURRIES. Nouns ending in J and X will be permitted an ES plural form unless otherwise indicated by the dictionary. For example, RAJ to RAJES and TAX to TAXES.

Verbs may be modified in three basic ways:

1. by the addition of S or ES (e.g. PICK to PICKS and TOUCH to TOUCHES). The addition of ES to a verb may also be accompanied by a change of a final Y to an I; for example, BURY to BURIES.

2. by the addition of D or ED (e.g. HOPE to HOPED and LAST to LASTED). A Y-to-I change or the doubling of a final consonant may also occur; for example, HURRY to HURRIED and ROT to ROTTED. The exceptions to this are where the dictionary specifies some other form of the past tense. For example, SWIM to SWAM and SWUM; and BURN to BURNED and BURNT.

3. by the addition of ING, with a possible dropping of a final E or the doubling of a final consonant. For example, GO to GOING; BURY to BURYING; STATE to STATING; and HOP to HOPPING. If a verb ends in UE and the ending is not clearly given by the dictionary, then the forms ending in UEING and UING will both be allowed. For example, TRUEING and TRUING are both allowed, because the dictionary lists neither of them; RUEING and RUING are both allowed because the dictionary lists both of them; and only SUING (not SUEING) is allowed because this is the only form shown in the dictionary.

No other forms of verbs will be allowed unless they are specifically shown in the dictionary. For example, DO to DOTH, LIST to LISTETH, RISE to ROSE, and SAY to SAYEST are all allowed, because they are all in the dictionary and none of them contravenes any of the other rules regarding acceptability.

Nouns ending in ING which are derived from verbs must be clearly marked by the dictionary as nouns if their plural forms are to be allowed. For example, the following are all shown by the dictionary to be nouns: BLUEING, GOING, LIKING and TAXING; accordingly, they can all have a plural formed by the addition of an S. But, none of the following is shown by the dictionary to be a noun: MATING, NOTING, PINING and RAPING; accordingly, none of them can be pluralised.

The addition of ER and EST to adjectives, to form comparatives and superlatives, is normally acceptable, whether or not the dictionary shows these forms. There may occasionally be a Y-to-I change, a doubling of a final consonant, or the dropping of an E. For example, CLEAN to CLEANER, GRAVE to GRAVEST, HAPPY to HAPPIEST, HOT to HOTTER, and WILY to WILIEST.

In spelling words, all accents may be ignored. For example, ÉLAN is to be treated as ELAN; FÊTE is to be treated as FETE; FÖHN is to be treated as FOHN; GARÇON is to be treated as GARCON; and so on.

A word which appears in the dictionary only as part of a multi-word phrase is not allowable. For example, APIEZON occurs only in the phrase APIEZON OILS; and FOLIC occurs only in the phrase FOLIC ACID. Accordingly, neither APIEZON nor FOLIC is acceptable. However, if the dictionary shows one or other of the words in brackets, indicating that the other word can stand alone, then this stand-alone word is allowable. For example, MORNAY (SAUCE) and PLATANNA (FROG) both appear in the dictionary. Accordingly, both MORNAY and PLATANNA are allowable, as are their plurals.

If these rules seem, at first sight, unnecessarily complicated, it just goes to show how seriously Scrabble players take the National Scrabble Championship. These rules *are* necessary. When the Championship can and does hinge on the allowability of one particular word, it is vital that such a properly thought-out set of rules exists, is known to the players, and is enforced.

3
Secrets of Success

How to become a Scrabble champion; a complete guide to becoming a first-class Scrabble player.

The High-Value Letters

The fifteen letters worth 4 or more points may be thought of as the 'high-value' letters. The letters, their point values, and distributions are given here:

letter	number in a set	point value
F	2	4
H	2	4
J	1	8
K	1	5
Q	1	10
V	2	4
W	2	4
X	1	8
Y	2	4
Z	1	10

To get the most from these letters, you should attempt to combine them with the premium score squares, effectively multiplying their face values. If you want to use a double-letter-score or triple-letter-score square, obviously the high-value letter must be placed on the premium square concerned. But for the double-word-score and triple-word-score squares, the high-value letter may occur anywhere in the word played, just so long as the word itself covers the premium square concerned. Much better even is to use a high-value letter on a double-letter-score or triple-letter-score square and also to make the whole word in which it appears cover a double-word-score or triple-word-score square. In this way, the face values of the high-value letters can be multiplied up even more. With the 'high-value' letters. The letters, their point values, and distributions medium-length words (that is, with three to five letters). Often there is little point in making a longer word unless it gives you a considerably higher score or it enables you to get rid of letters from your rack that you don't want. Elsewhere in this book is a complete list of all the three-letter words from *Chambers Twentieth Century Dictionary* (with 1977 Supplement) that are allowable under the rules of the National Scrabble Championship. There are also lists of words that have four or five letters and which have one or more of the four highest value letters, JQXZ. Again, all of the words in these lists are allowable under the rules of the National Scrabble Championship. Here is a small collection of four and five-letter words which use at least two of the letters FHKVWY. You are bound to be able to think of others to add to these lists.

ASHY	FLAY	KAYF	RUKH	WALK
AVOW	FOWL	KERF	SHAW	WAVY
AWRY	FROW	KITH	SHIV	WHOW
AYAH	FURY	KIWI	SWAY	WIVE
ENVY	HALF	KNEW	THEW	WOWF
EYRY	HATH	LAWK	TOWY	YAFF
FAKE	HEWN	NAVY	VERY	YAWN
FIEF	HIVE	NOWY	VIEW	YERK
FIVE	HOVE	OAKY	VINY	YEUK
FLAW	HOWL	OWLY	WAIF	YOKE

ASKEW	EWHOW	HOOEY	LEAFY	SHAKY
ASWAY	FAERY	HOWFF	NARKY	SKIVY
AWAKE	FAITH	HUFFY	NEWLY	SWANK
AWASH	FAKER	HULKY	NIFTY	THEWY
AWAVE	FATLY	IVORY	OFFAL	VEERY
AWFUL	FERNY	KEEVE	RAWLY	VIEWY
ENVOY	FETWA	KOTOW	RAYAH	VINYL
ETHYL	FEVER	KYTHE	REIFY	VROUW
EVERY	FLYER	LARKY	ROOKY	WAVEY
EVOKE	FUNKY	LAWNY	ROWTH	YARFA

If you do find yourself with several of the high-value letters and there is no way that you can use any of them on a premium square, what should you do? The best bet is to use the letters as quickly as possible, scoring as many points as you can. If you can't use any premium square, so be it. Some players would suggest that you hold on to the high-value letters hoping that an opportunity to use a premium square will arise in the next few turns. Generally, this is misguided, though occasionally there may be exceptions. Players who advocate this approach tend to believe that high-value letters make high scores and the other letters make low scores. While this is probably true for novices, it just isn't true for advanced players. The advanced player will usually manage to use his lower-value letters for a much higher score ultimately. The advice given here is this: if you are holding high-value letters and there are no premium squares that you can use, get rid of the letters as soon as possible, hoping that you will pick up more useful letters for your next turn. This is particularly true for FJKQVXZ, which are not quite so versatile as HWY. After all, there is little point in waiting for three or four turns to get your Q on a triple-letter-score if in the meantime you have scored a mere handful of points on each of your turns.

Having offered this advice, though, you will find that there are occasionally genuine exceptions to it. Ultimately, you must assess whether it is worth playing a high-value letter now for less points than you might get if you played it later on. How many points are you likely to score while you are waiting? How long will you have to wait? Is your opponent likely to use the premium squares that you have got your eye on anyway? And so on.

Premium Squares

Playing Scrabble well and scoring highly require that you must always be aware of the relative values of different premium squares, the letters on your rack, and their possible combinations. Before putting down the first word that springs to mind, do look for the alternatives. How many points would you get from each of

Figure 30

them? Though one may score more highly than another, it might use letters that you would rather hang on to for a while. If you want to take the lower-scoring move, by all means do. Just be aware of all the options, though. Consider the example shown in Figure 30. The words LAME and IRE are already on the board, and you have the letters AEFKLRY on your rack. Your first thought might be to use the I of IRE and the letters FARY from your rack to make the word FAIRY. This has both the F and the Y covering triple-letter-score squares, and is worth a total of 27 points. With a little more thought you might have seen FLAKE and FIRE (with the F in front of IRE) for 31 points. Using the A of LAME and the letters FLKY from your rack, you could put down FLAKY for 31 points. Again, the F and Y both cover triple-letter-score squares. Having spotted FLAKY, you might then consider repositioning it so that the F comes in front of IRE. This would cover a double-word-score square, and the total score is 37 points. If you spotted the double-letter-score square in front of LAME, you would have thought of FLAME and a possible five-letter word stretching down to the F or down from the F, so that it covered a double-word-score square. FLAKE and FLAME would be worth 46 points; but FLAKY and FLAME would be worth 52 points. The moral: look before you leap! Other possibilities which you ought to have seen, and rejected, are these: using the L of LAME and FAKY from your rack, make FLAKY for 30 points; using the L of LAME and the letters ALKY from your rack, make the word ALKYL across either of the two double-word-score squares for 24 points. Also, in passing, you should have considered using the I of IRE and all seven of your letters to make the word FREAKILY, with the A and the Y falling on the triple-letter-score squares. This would be worth a magnificent 78 points. (Don't forget that there is a 50-point bonus for using all seven of your letters at one turn.) Because FREAKILY isn't in Chambers dictionary you might have been wary of using it. In fact, it is allowable because Chambers lists FREAKY and the championship rules permit the use of adverbial forms of allowable adjectives whether these are listed or not.

Figure 31

Figure 31 offers another illustrative example. The words AT, RADIO, TROPHY, HE and EARLY are already on the board. On your rack are the letters DEHKOPY. Before putting down any letters at all, enumerate the possibilities. Here are some of them:

PIKE (18 points); POKY (21 points); HOOKED (24 points); HOPED, HI and OO (28 points); POKED and EAT (31 points); YOKED and EAT (33 points); PEEKED (38 points); POKED and HEP (47 points); YOKED and HEY (51 points); POKED and DEARLY (54 points); YOKED and DEARLY (57 points); POKY and PEARLY (59 points); YOKE and YEARLY (61 points); DOPEY and YEARLY (61 points).

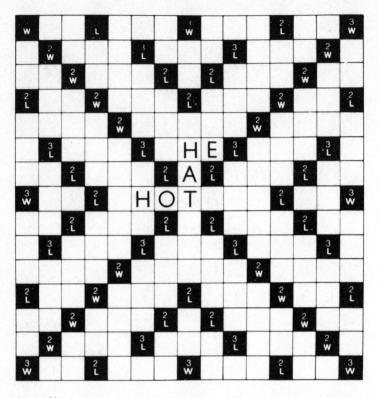

Figure 32

The last five of these demonstrate that you should always be on the lookout for premium squares that can be used in two directions at the same time, especially when one of the words involved also covers a double-word-score or triple-word-score square.

Figure 32 offers yet another example. The words HE, HAT and HOT are already on the board, and on your rack are the letters **AESTWXY**. Yet again, list off the various possibilities before placing any letters on the board. Here are some of the possibilities in this case:

WAXES and SHOT (37 points); WAX, HA and OX (43 points); WAXY, WHAT and AE (46 points); WAX, WO and EX (51 points); WAXES, HA, OX and HATE (53 points); WAXY, WO and EX (55 points); WAXY and HEX (62 points).

Be especially on the lookout for triple-letter-score squares like the one in this example when you have high-value letters. The score can really mount up when a high-value letter is tripled in two words.

What to Do with the Q

Many Scrabble players just don't know how to handle the Q properly. If you treat it right, you can get good scores from it; if you misuse it, you will find yourself in trouble. All the allowable words in Chambers which have a Q also have a U immediately afterwards, with one exception. MUQADDAM (an Arabic headman) is shown in the dictionary, and even that has a U elsewhere in the word. To all intents and purposes, then, you can assume that you will need a U, or a blank, to go with your Q. When you first pick up the Q, determine how many Us are already on the board and how many are left to come. If any one of the Us on the board is in a position such that you can use it in conjunction with your U, then do so straightaway. Don't be too bothered that you have not managed to play your word on some premium square. Just be pleased that you have got rid of the Q without too many problems. If your word does manage to cover a premium square, well, so much the better.

Many players feel that the Q is a valuable letter to have because of its 10-point face value. These players dislike using the Q for anything less than big scores, and this is where they come unstuck. They will hold on to the Q for several turns until they manage to pick up a U or a blank, and then they will wait until a triple-letter-score square presents itself for them to put their Q on. They may well wait for six or seven turns, just to triple their Q. Meanwhile, their opponent is forging ahead! If, while holding on to the Q and waiting for a U to appear, a player can make some reasonable interim scores (say, 25 to 35 points for each turn), then this can be justified.

If you have the Q, all the Us have been played, and none of them can be used in conjunction with your Q, what do you do? Exchange the Q. Put it back in the pool of unused letters and select a replacement. This is the time to be ruthless. This will invariably be your best option, especially if the end of the game is near and there is a good chance of your opponent getting stuck with the Q. Even in situations where there are still Us to be played, you would be well advised to consider exchanging the Q, along with any other undesirable letters on your rack. Once you have put the Q back, there is the possibility that you will pick it up again. Even so, you should still seriously think about exchanging the horrid letter.

Chambers has only one three-letter word using the Q (it is QUA). All the four and five letter words from Chambers which have a Q and which would be allowable at the National Scrabble Championship are included in the lists of words having the letters JQXZ elsewhere in this book. Do try and memorise some of them.

Of course, if you are fortunate enough to have a Q and a U together on your rack, you are recommended to try and use them as soon as possible. As before, look carefully at the board, and enumerate the alternatives. Only when you are sure that you have found the best move should you actually start putting your letters on the board.

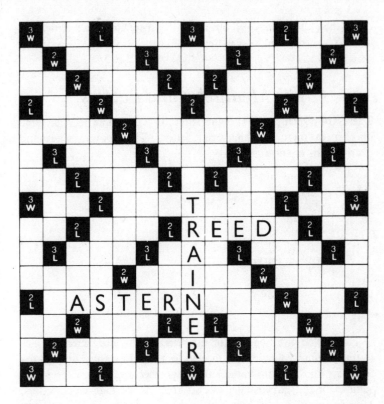

Figure 33

Figure 33 offers an illustrative example. The words TRAINER, REED and ASTERN are already on the board, and your letters are ENQRSUY. Here are the options:

> QUERY and REEDY (27 points); QUEST (28 points);
> QUA (32 points); QUAY (32 points); QUEER (36 points);
> QUERNS and REEDS (38 points); QUEAN (48 points);
> QUERY and EASTERN (81 points); QUEYS and
> TRAINERS (105 points)

If you don't know words like, QUERN, QUEAN and QUEY, look

them up in Chambers, find out what they mean, and then remember them. You are bound to need them.

The Medium-value Letters

There are fifteen medium-value letters in a Scrabble set, the same number as there are high-value letters. Their point values and distributions are given here:

letter	number in a set	point value
B	2	3
C	2	3
D	4	2
G	3	2
M	2	3
P	2	3

The advice given earlier for the fifteen high-value letters applies to the medium-value letters, though to a lesser extent. The rewards for using the medium-value letters, whether they fall on premium squares or not, are usually not so great as for high-value letters. Many times there will be no great point in striving to make a play which just ends up with a G, say, on a double-letter-score square. However, do watch out for combinations of premium squares when you have medium-value letters. If you can double the point value of a letter and then double or even triple the score for the whole word, that can be well worth doing.

The medium-value letters cannot be considered in isolation, though. There will be many occasions when you have to use them in combination with the high-value letters and the low-value letters. Here are two lists of words, having four letters and five letters, that use low-value, medium-value and high-value letters. All the words are in Chambers, and all would be allowable at the National

Scrabble Championship.

ABYE	CHUM	GYVE	PALY	SKIP
AHEM	DAWK	HAWM	PAWK	SOWP
BABY	DERV	HOMY	PHEW	SPEW
BATH	DEWY	KERB	POKY	TIDY
BEVY	DHAK	LACY	PUNK	TYPE
BOGY	DYNE	LIMY	RICY	UMPH
BOOK	ECHO	MICK	RUCK	UPBY
CHEZ	FADY	MONK	RYPE	WRAP
CHIV	GAWP	OBEY	SCRY	YACK
CHOW	GOWF	OPAH	SHIM	YAUP
BARKY	CETYL	GAWKY	MUCKY	THUMB
BATIK	CHAMP	GHYLL	NYMPH	TYPTO
BENDY	CHINE	HOMEY	OGIVE	UNKED
BHANG	CRAPY	HYLEG	PARKY	VARDY
BITCH	CYDER	IMPLY	PIGMY	VELDT
BLIMY	DEIFY	ITCHY	PYLON	WHELM
BOOKY	DOGGY	LIMEY	RETCH	WISPY
BRAVO	DWARF	MACAW	RUGBY	YERBA
CACHE	EMBOW	MATEY	SPEWY	YOBBO
CAVEL	EPHOD	MUFTI	SPOOF	YOICK

The Low-value Letters

In addition to the fifteen high-value letters and the fifteen medium-value letters, there are 70 others, 68 of them worth just one point, and two of them blanks. As 70 per cent of the letters are worth one point or less, players cannot expect to pick up high-value and medium-value letters throughout the game. Neither should they expect to make the bulk of their final score from the high-value and medium-value letters. How then is the player meant to handle the 70 low-value letters? How are they to be played so as to get high scores from them? Simply, by playing for the 50-point bonus.

Playing for the Bonus

To get high scores, you need to score 50-point bonuses by putting down all seven of your letters several times over. An expert player will often manage two or three bonuses in a game, and even six or seven bonuses on the part of one player is not unknown! Very rarely do bonuses just fall into your lap. They have to be worked at.

Even if you manage to see a seven-letter word from the letters on your rack, there is no guarantee that there will be any position on the board where the word can be played. And even if you can see somewhere to get your word down, look for the alternatives. There may be better places for your word to go; better in the sense that you might score more points, or better in the sense that the board might become more 'open'. Before putting your letters on the board, calculate the scores that are available to you. Just because you can see where you can score 72 points, say, you cannot afford to ignore the possibility that a position exists which would score you 85 points.

Even though you may be unable to see a word on your rack, you might well be able to use a letter already on the board to make an eight-letter word. Many novice players concentrate on looking for seven-letter words on their racks, and only afterwards do they look for somewhere to play them. The accomplished player is considering both the letters on his rack and the layout of the board. He is thinking about the positions on the board where a seven-letter word could go, often before he has even spotted the word on his rack, and he is also pondering on the letters on the board which could be combined with those on his rack. He looks for free, available letters, and then begins to think whether any of them will combine with his seven letters.

Figure 34

Figure 34 illustrates the point that various different positions on the board have to be looked at. The words JUNTA, RAIN, ON and ILL are already on the board, and you are holding AGINSTY on your rack. You will, of course, have managed to see the word STAYING. Now look for the various places where the word will go. Firstly, the G or T could go on the front of RAIN, making GRAIN or TRAIN. GRAIN and STAYING is worth 71 points; and TRAIN and STAYING is worth 74 points. But RAIN can also take an S or a Y at its end, making RAINS or RAINY.

You could play RAINS and STAYING for 77 points. Unfortunately, you cannot play RAINY and STAYING, the latter across two double-word-score squares, because you would also have to make the sequence OA, and that isn't a word. You could put the S of STAYING on the end of ILL, making ILLS. This gets STAYING across a double-word-score square, and is worth 76 points. This is a particularly unattractive move as it opens up for your opponent the two triple-word-score squares in the rightmost column of the board. If he managed to make an eight-letter word stretching across both these premium squares, that would be bad news for you. Another alternative is to put the Y of STAYING at the end of ILL, making ILLY. This is worth 79 points. (If ILLY is a new word to you, just add it to your growing repertoire of useful words.) Can 79 points be bettered? What letters are there on the board which you might be able to combine with your letters? There's the second L of ILL, the J of JUNTA, the U of JUNTA, possibly the N of JUNTA, and the R of RAIN. The J seems unlikely, but should not be dismissed out of hand. Dismiss it only when you are certain that you cannot use it. The U of JUNTA is a particularly attractive possibility. If there is an eight-letter word with the U in the fourth or fifth position, then two double-word-score squares would be covered. Similarly, if there was another word, apart from STAYING, with the S or the Y in the fifth position, so that ILLS or ILLY could be made, then this could be played across two double-word-score squares, too. A last possibility hinges on RAINS or RAINY. Is there a seven-letter word with an S or Y in the fourth position, and having its third letter combining with the O of ON to make a valid two-letter word? If so, it could be played across two double-word-score squares. Continued racking of brains throws up no words at all that satisfy any of these conditions. Accordingly, ILLY and STAYING are played for 79 points. Notice the way the expert player's mind is working here. He is not so concerned about the letters on his rack; he is identifying places on the board where words would go, and then seeing how his letters can be fitted into these positions.

Figure 35

Figure 35 illustrates the point about making eight-letter words, using a letter already on the board in combination with the letters on your rack. The words CABLING, ARGOT, FIDDLE, OF, TIRO, SO, SLOOP, PEN, PHANTOM, ENDING, TOIL and GO are already on the board. On your rack are the letters AEINRST. You should have seen words such as NASTIER, RETAINS and RETINAS from the outset. Once you have become familiar with the lists presented elsewhere in this book, you will know that RATINES, RESIANT, RETSINA, STAINER, STARNIE and

STEARIN are also words that can be made from the letters you have. The accomplished Scrabble player will know all of these, and will dredge them from the back of his mind once he sees the AEINRST combination in his rack. The possibilities open to you are numerous. Here are just a few using seven-letter words:

RETAINS and TOILS (69 points); RETINAS and TOILS (69 points); NASTIER and RENDING (70 points); RETAINS and SENDING (70 points); RETINAS and SENDING (70 points); NASTIER, IN and LA (74 points); NASTIER and TENDING (77 points); NASTIER and SLOOPS (83 points)

But what about eight-letter words? The possibilities are rife. Here are a few of them, below. You may well be able to see others. The P of SLOOP could be used to make PAINTERS, PANTRIES or PERTAINS, all for 64 points; or the same P could be used to make REPAINTS for a slightly better 72 points. The second O of SLOOP could be used to make NOTARIES, for 70 points. The R of ARGOT could be used to make RESTRAIN, for 70 points. The first N of ENDING could be used to make ENTRAINS, for 59 points. The second D of FIDDLE would help to make STRAINED, for 61 points. The B of CABLING would help to make BANISTER, for 62 points. The E of ENDING would help to make TRAINEES, for 70 points. The L of TOIL could contribute to ENTRAILS, worth 68 points; notice that the word PEN, already on the board, would be turned into PENT here. The C of CABLING could contribute to SCANTIER, stretching across a triple-word-score square and making 80 points. The M of PHANTOM could be incorporated into either MINARETS or RAIMENTS, both worth 83 points. The D of ENDING could be included in STRAINED, covering two double-word-score squares and scoring 86 points. The A of ARGOT can be used to make ARTESIAN. If the A becomes the initial letter of ARTESIAN, you will score 77 points. But, if the A of ARGOT becomes the second A of ARTESIAN, you will get ARTESIAN stretching across two triple-word-score squares, which will be worth a massive 131 points! An even better position exists on the board, if only you could think of a word to put down. If you could come up with an eight-letter word having M as its seventh letter, you could put the word down across the two triple-word-score squares in the rightmost column. That would score 149 points. So, don't just concentrate on the letters on your rack. Look at the board. See what letters are available, and work out whether they can be combined with the letters on your rack. This won't always work, but when it can, make sure that you don't miss the opportunity.

Making the Bonus Words

Unless you actually work to achieve your 50-point bonuses, you are most unlikely to get them. Only very rarely will a bonus word appear by accident on your rack. How then should you go about getting bonuses? What do you have to do to make them happen?

The simplest way is to hold on to the easy-to-use letters, those worth one or two points, and the blanks, of course. Try to avoid having duplicates of letters, perhaps making an exception for Es and Ss. Two of either of these letters won't cause you too many problems, but two Ns or two Us may well be difficult to handle. Use up your duplicate letters as quickly as you can. Play them on the board in conjunction with the high-value letters which you are striving to get rid of; or return them to the pool of unused letters at the same time that you return your unwanted Q and two Vs! For example, with the letters AAEENRT on your rack, you would be wise to play the duplicate A and E somewhere on the board. AE and EA are both allowable two-letter words, so you should be able to dump the two letters quite easily. If you have to choose between vowels when deciding what to discard, ditch Os and Us in preference to As, Es and Is. For example, with AAIOOUU on your rack, if you can only get rid of two letters, use up the duplicate O and U, rather than A and O, or A and U. Better still, think about exchanging five or six of the tiles and getting some new ones from the pool. When getting shot of unwanted Us, consider where the Q might be first and how many Us are already on the board. You don't want to dump the last U only to pick up the Q!

When aiming for bonuses, you should try to have two or three vowels on your rack only, and do get rid of those high-value letters as fast as you can. They do so restrict your opportunities for bonus scores. With a rack of letters such as AKNOOTT, you should try to play TOOK (or even KOTO, which is a word) somewhere, leaving you with ANT, a nice group of three letters.

Remember that the number of vowels (including Ys) is 46, and that the number of consonants is 52. In other words, there are more or less equal numbers of both. When you pick up new letters from the pool, you will tend to pick up an equal number of vowels and consonants. If you pick up an odd number of letters, the split will usually be as close to equal as is possible for the number concerned. Do be prepared for vowels and consonants to come out of the central pool in roughly equal quantities. There's little point in playing RANT from a rack containing AAEINRT, leaving yourself with AEI, and then being surprised when you get two more vowels in your new letters. If possible, play the duplicate A only, and then you won't be too bothered whether a vowel or a consonant comes out of the pool when you take your new letter. Another example: given the letters AADEEII on your rack, you might decide to get rid of the duplicate letters, AEI. But to do this, you will probably have to use your only consonant, making the word IDEA somewhere on the board. This leaves you with AEI. Picking up four new tiles will, on most occasions, lead you to holding five vowels and two consonants. And you will still have your excess vowel problems! In this situation, you would be best advised to return your unwanted letters to the pool of unused ones and to pick some replacement letters. Either return AEI (leaving you with ADEI) or, probably fractionally better, return AAEI (leaving you with DEI). Returning AEI still leaves you with a 3-to-1 vowel-consonant split, and there could easily be two more vowels in the three letters you pick up; this would leave you with a 5-to-2 vowel-consonant split. The better move, putting back AAEI, leaves you with a fairly balanced rack, DEI. Why put back both

As rather than both Es or both Is? Because the sequence DEI seems potentially easier to handle than ADE or ADI. Given that you started with the letters AADEEII, it probably isn't a good idea to return five letters (AAEII) to the pool and pick five new ones. You must remember that the more new letters you select from the pool, the greater are your chances of picking out an undesirable letter (another vowel, the Q, or one of the other high-value letters). Keep your letters balanced and under control. The randomness of the pool, induced by all the shaking and the mixing which it gets, will only serve to imbalance your hand. And you want to introduce into your hand as little randomising influence as possible. And you can do that by keeping down the number of letters which you exchange.

Never start off with the idea of making one specific word, even though you may have six of its seven letters. This is so often the start of the road to failure, where, for three or four moves, you are hoping to pick up a solitary D, or a T, or even an E, and you struggle along making insignificant scores all the while that you are hoping.

The attraction of the one and two-point letters is that they can be combined in so many ways with each other. The implication of this is that if you retain your letters in a sensible manner (concentrating on the low-value letters, avoiding duplicated letters, and keeping a reasonable balance between vowels and consonants), then you will fairly soon get the chance of playing all seven of your letters. Just look at these seven-letter words, all of them using one and two-point letters. There are many more that you will undoubtedly be able to add to this short list. This little group should prove to you how easy it is to make seven-letter words from the letters worth one and two points.

ALIGNED	ERASING	IGNORED	NEAREST
ANGLERS	ENTRIES	INSERTS	NESTING
DARTING	GANDERS	LINGERS	ORATION
DEAREST	GRANITE	LOITERS	OUTSIDE

READING	SEALING	TOADIES	UNTRIED
ROUSING	STAINER	TRAINED	URINATE

Suppose that on your rack you have the letters AEIRSTY. You should play the Y. Put it down for the best score you can, but be prepared to accept five points if necessary. With your next pick-up, you are almost certain to get a letter that will combine with the AEIRST on your rack to make a seven-letter word. Watch out for these groups of six letters which combine well with other letters. For example, AEIRST combines with 20 other different letters (*not* JQUXYZ), and these 20 other letters account for 90 per cent of the tiles in the game. Elsewhere in this book you will find a list of all the words that can be made by adding a single letter to AEIRST. You will also find 49 similar lists, a total of 50, for six-letter groups such as AEERST, AEINST, AENRST, EGINRT and EINRST. Browse through the 50 lists. You don't have to learn all the words off by heart, though many enthusiastic players do know most of the words. Get some idea of the six-letter groups that you should try and get on your rack, and learn as many of the words in the lists as you can. Then, when you have, say, DEENRS on your rack, and you pick up a Z as your seventh letter, you won't be at loss as to what to do. You will immediately recall the strange-looking word DZERENS which is included in the lists. Of course, having found the word on your rack, you may run into one or two problems about putting it down on the board somewhere. As you become more familiar with the words in the 50 lists, you will realise that bonuses are not necessarily always achieved by using the one and two-point letters. All the letters, medium-value and high-value, can be used in bonus words, as long as you have the right letters with which to combine them. Seasoned Scrabble players are no longer surprised at the regularity with which a word like ANTIQUE (or even its anagram QUINATE) comes up. This is because the Q is in combination with easy-to-use, single-point letters. Much more surprising would be to see a word like QUICKLY played, having, as it does, a Q, C, K and Y!

Common Letter-groups

When juggling with the letters on your rack, to see if you can make a word, it may help you if you bear in mind some of the groups of letters which frequently occur together. Here are 50 of the commonest ones:

-ANCE	-ENCE	-IED	-IST	OUT-
-ANT	-ENT	-IER	-IUM	OVER-
-ARY	-ER	-IES	-IUS	PRE-
-ATE	-ERY	-IEST	-IZE	PRO-
-ATOR	-EST	-INE	-LY	RE-
-CK-	EX-	-ING	-MAN	-TCH-
DE-	-GHT-	-ION	-MEN	-TH-
DIS-	-IAL	-IOUS	-ORY	-UM
-ED	-IAN	-ISE	-OUR	UN-
EN-	-IC	-ISM	-OUS	-URE

Bonuses from Blanks

Though the two blanks have no point values, they are the two most valuable tiles in the whole game. In a two-player game, it is generally unwise to play a blank for a score of less than 50 points during the first two-thirds of a game. If you follow the advice already given (about sticking to the one and two-point letters, having no duplicated letters, and having a balanced vowel-consonant split), then, with a blank on your rack, you will usually be very close to getting a bonus. To use the blank tiles to score 30-40 points may well lose you 70-80 points a couple of moves later. Using the blanks to score 15-30 points as quite a few novices do, is a waste, with the end-game situation being an exception. If the end of a game is in sight, you have a blank on your rack, and you suspect that your opponent is about to go out fairly quickly, you may have to use the blank for 10-20 points; for example, by using it as an S and pluralising some noun already on the board. This is a pity, but there isn't usually any alternative. Occasionally, though, a player will hold a blank right at the end of a game and manage to put down a seven-letter word. There aren't many games which are open enough at the end to allow for a seven-letter word to go down.

High Scores from Blanks

In the first two-thirds of a game, you should have no hesitation in using a blank for a total of around 50 points, even though you may not get a 50-point bonus. That is, you may score about 50 points but not use up all seven of your tiles. Figure 36 illustrates an example. The words ASPIC, CORAL, LAC and AX are already on the board, and you have EHKRRT and a blank on your rack. You should turn LAC into LACK and make the word KART vertically, using the blank as an A, so that it covers the triple-word-score square in the board's bottom right-hand corner. This scores 51 points, and leaves you with HER. Using the blank as an I, you could have played HIKER and AXE. This would score 48 points, and leave you with RT. There isn't much to choose between these two moves, though the former is marginally better. Why, since it leaves you with a high-value letter, the H? H is usually a fairly easy letter to use, and the other two letters, ER, aren't going to cause you any problems. If you had been left with something like FER or VER, then the 48 points move might have been the better one, even though it scores three points less.

One other point, concerning the Q and blank together. If you have a Q, a blank, but no U, what should you do? This is one situation where it might be worth using the blank as a U to score upwards of 30 points. If you cannot play the Q and blank for at least this sort of score, put the Q back in the pool and choose another letter. On most occasions, it is not wise to use the blank as a U just to get rid of the Q and score less than 30 points.

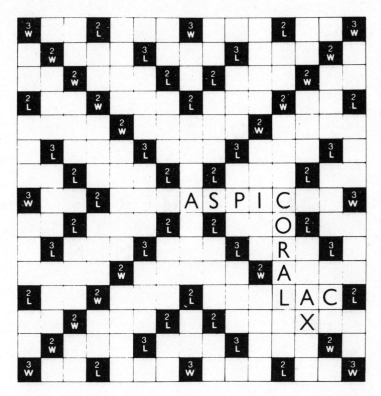

Figure 36

Two-letter Words

The overwhelming importance of two-letter words and their proper use cannot be sufficiently emphasised. Many novice players who have not read the official Scrabble rules carefully enough believe that two-letter words are not allowable. They are wrong. Nowhere do the official rules bar the use of two-letter words. Such words, as short as they are, are perfectly acceptable in Scrabble, as long as they contravene none of the other various rules. Two-letter words are important, usually not for the scores which they make themselves, but for the scores of the other words formed at the same time.

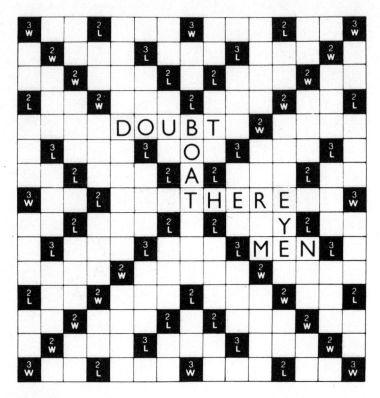

Figure 37

Consider the example shown in Figure 37. The words DOUBT, BOAT, THERE, EYE and MEN are already on the board. Your turn is next, and on your rack you have EILMOPR. Are you able to make a word from these letters? And if so, where will you put it? You should be able to see IMPLORE easily enough, but is there room to put it down on the board? There are two possibilities, both involving the use of two-letter words. Using the T of DOUBT, you could make IT vertically and IMPLORE horizontally, scoring 76 points. Or, even better, you could use the M of MEN to make ME vertically and IMPLORE horizontally. ME covers one double-word-score square, and IMPLORE covers two double-word-score squares. The total score here is a very healthy 102 points. Two-letter words are very frequently used to add seven-letter words to the board in this way.

Some inexperienced players will only ever use such everyday two-letter words as AN, DO, HE, IT, SO and WE. Experienced players will use any of the allowable two-letter words that are to be found in the dictionary which they are using. In *Chambers Twentieth Century Dictionary*, there are 86 two-letter words that are allowed at the National Scrabble Championship. A full list of them is given elsewhere in this book. The list also includes their parts of speech (is it a noun? is it a verb? is it an interjection?) and their meanings. Some of the more esoteric words listed in Chambers are given here:

AE	GU	LI	UG
DA	IO	MO	WO
EA	JO	NA	YU
FY	KA	OB	ZO

Experienced players will be able to tell you immediately what these all mean, whether they can be pluralised or not, and so on.

The two-letter words that occur in different dictionaries vary to an astonishing degree. The number of words offered by a dictionary is generally in proportion to its size. So, the bigger the dictionary, the more two-letter words it is likely to contain. Given below are a few two-letter words that can be found in other dictionaries, but which are not in Chambers.

AA is a type of volcanic lava
AW is an interjection
DY is a type of sediment found in lakes
HM is an interjection
IE is a pine
KI is a tree found in the Pacific
OM is a mystical Hindu chant
PO is a chamber-pot
XU is a Vietnamese coin
YI is a term from Chinese philosophy

To reiterate, none of these is in Chambers, and none would be allowed at the National Scrabble Championship. They should give you some idea of the diversity which exists between different dictionaries, though.

The abundance of two-letter words also helps in getting rid of your unwanted letters faster than you otherwise might. Knowing that KY is an allowable two-letter word (a strange plural of 'cow') might help you in dumping an unwanted K and Y. There are other occasions when two-letter words can score very highly in their own right. Consider the example shown in Figure 38. On your rack are the letters BFHKMXZ, not a particularly desirable set! Your choices are many.

Using the A of PAL and the first A of ALWAYS, you could make MA and MA (20 points), or FA and FA (26 points), or HA and HA (26 points), or KA and KA (32 points); using the Y of DAYS and the Y of ALWAYS, you could make MY and MY (26 points), or FY and FY (32 points), or KY and KY (38 points); using the E of COMET and the O of MOB, you could make EH and OH (26 points), or EX and OX (50 points); and using the O of COD and the O of POD, you could make BO and BO (20 points), or MO and MO (20 points), or HO and HO (26 points), or ZO and ZO (62 points). Take the 62-point score. Then, if your opponent doesn't spoil it, take the 50-point score on your next turn. Continue picking off the triple-letter-score squares as long as you can.

Figure 38

Figure 39

Figure 39 illustrates the case of an eight-letter word being played and depending on several two-letter words. You have the letters ADEENRT on your rack. Those letters by themselves do not make a word. What to do? Play an E somewhere for a few points? Or exchange the E and get a replacement from the pool? Neither! Use the I of IS in the top row and make the eight-letter word RETAINED. At the same time, you will make RE, EX, TI, EM, DA and ATOLL. The net score is 176 points! But it couldn't have been done without those valuable two-letter words.

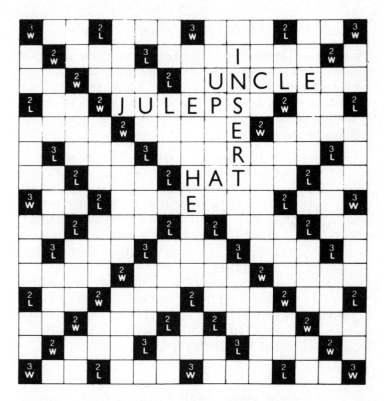

Figure 40

Figure 40 illustrates a similar situation, but not involving such a high score. The words INSERT, UNCLE, UP, JULEPS, HAT and HE are already on the board, and on your rack are the letters GIINNOY. You would like to get rid of the duplicate I and N; and you would also like to use the Y. While YIN is a word (a Scots form of 'one'), the best that you can score with it is 17 points, by making YE at the same time, using the E of UNCLE. Much better is to play YOGIN, underneath and parallel to JULEPS, making JO, UG, LI and EN at the same time. This scores 43 points. Using the G and O for the extra 26 points is well worth it.

Modifying Words

Once a word is on the board, it can be modified by the addition of one or more letters in front of the word (prefixing), or after the word (suffixing), or by both together. Given here are some examples of modified words. The words on the left can be thought of as being already on the board, and those on the right are what they may be modified to give.

GO	GOT, GONE, GOING, GOLDEN, AGO, SAGO, TANGO, STINGO, AGOG, AGONY, EGOIST, EGOTIST, ARGON, ZYGOTE, ONGOING, ARGONAUT, UNDERGONE
EAR	EARN, EARLY, EARTHY, EARNEST, BEAR, SPEAR, LINEAR, NUCLEAR, PEARLY, SHEARED, DREARILY, HEARTFELT
LINK	LINKS, LINKED, LINKING, LINKAGES, CLINK, SLINKY, UNLINKED, BLINKERED
EARTH	EARTHY, EARTHEN, EARTHING, EARTHLING, DEARTH, UNEARTHED, INEARTHING

Prefixing with One Letter

This is where just one letter is added to the beginning of a word already on the board. It is very important, and for the same reason that two-letter words are important. Namely, in making a word perpendicular to the word that is being prefixed. The new word formed by prefixing doesn't usually score that highly, but the word formed perpendicularly can and usually does score well.

Figure 41

Figure 41 illustrates an example. The words BASH and WAKE are already on the board, and you have the letters AEILLST on your rack. After shuffling your letters for a while, you spot TALLIES. You cannot pluralise BASH by the addition of a single S. You cannot make WAKES and TALLIES because there isn't enough room to get TALLIES in. You have just two opportunities. Using the A of TALLIES, turn WAKE into AWAKE (for 75 points), or using the same A, turn BASH into ABASH (for 77 points). The experienced Scrabble player knows a large number of words that can be modified by the prefixing of a single letter. For instance, he will certainly know that AI (a sloth) can be modified to give SAI (a monkey) and TAI (a fish). He knows that the word OO can be modified by a single-letter prefix to give BOO, COO, DOO (a dove), GOO, LOO, MOO, TOO, WOO and ZOO. Here are one hundred examples of words that can be modified by the addition of one letter. The added letter is shown in brackets.

(A)BET	(E)MOVE	(L)OUR	(S)CAD
(A)BYE	(E)NOW	(M)EASE	(S)CRY
(A)EON	(E)TWEE	(M)ETHYL	(S)ILEX
(A)HA	(E)VET	(N)ACRE	(S)LEE
(A)HEM	(F)LAG	(N)EON	(T)ALAR
(A)IT	(F)ROW	(N)EWT	(T)ALMA
(A)NA	(G)LADY	(N)IDE	(T)HEW
(A)POD	(G)LEG	(N)OILS	(T)IT
(A)TOP	(G)RIP	(N)UNDINE	(T)OFT
(B)AH	(H)AVER	(O)BIT	(T)WEE
(B)ILL	(H)EXARCH	(O)GAM	(U)PEND
(C)ERE	(I)BIS	(O)GEE	(U)RATE
(C)ORE	(I)CON	(O)LID	(U)REAL
(D)ALE	(I)DEAL	(O)PAH	(U)RENT
(D)ILL	(I)GAD	(O)PINE	(V)AGUE
(D)RAFT	(I)MAGE	(O)RANG	(V)ARE
(D)ZO	(I)ON	(O)VINE	(W)ALE
(E)DUCE	(I)RADE	(P)AEON	(W)RACK
(E)DUCT	(I)RATE	(P)EON	(X)YLEM
(E)GAD	(I)SH	(R)ACHE	(Y)ARE
(E)GO	(J)UNTO	(R)AIT	(Y)EAN
(E)LAND	(K)ART	(R)AND	(Z)AMBO
(E)LOIN	(L)AMP	(R)EAST	(Z)ANTE
(E)MIR	(L)AVER	(R)ELATE	(Z)EL
(E)MOTE	(L)EAT	(R)OOP	(Z)HO

You are bound to be able to think of plenty of others to add to this list.

94

Suffixing with One Letter

The object of suffixing with one letter is the same as that of prefixing with a single letter. Namely, to allow you to play a word perpendicularly to a word already on the board, modifying the word already on the board by adding a letter to its end. Just as all the letters except Q can be used for prefixing, so too can they all be used for suffixing, Q again being the exception. The experienced Scrabble player knows a large number of these words. For example, he is well aware that BE can be suffixed to give BED, BEE, BEG, BEL (a measure of sound), BEN, BET, BEY (a Turkish governor), and BEZ (part of a deer's horn). Here are 100 examples of words that can be modified by the addition of one letter. The added letter is shown in brackets.

COCO(A)	APOD(E)	TAX(I)	HER(O)
EROTIC(A)	FAD(E)	WAD(I)	OH(O)
GAG(A)	HOP(E)	YET(I)	QUART(O)
GAL(A)	JAK(E)	BEN(J)	TAR(O)
LOT(A)	LOT(E)	HAD(J)	WIN(O)
MAN(A)	SKYR(E)	DAW(K)	CAR(P)
OCHRE(A)	ULNA(E)	BEDE(L)	TAM(P)
VILL(A)	ULNAR(E)	EROTICA(L)	DEE(R)
VIOL(A)	SCAR(F)	HOVE(L)	LOVE(R)
JAM(B)	SCUR(F)	MIL(L)	TEA(R)
LAM(B)	KIN(G)	NOR(M)	ULNA(R)
MAGI(C)	RAISIN(G)	WAR(M)	VILLA(R)
MANIA(C)	RAN(G)	AIR(N)	WRITE(R)
AMEN(D)	PEC(H)	CANTO(N)	NEEDLES(S)
BAN(D)	PEG(H)	FIR(N)	PAS(S)
LAR(D)	CAD(I)	PEE(N)	PRINCES(S)
WAR(D)	IAMB(I)	TEE(N)	WINDLES(S)
AGE(E)	MAG(I)	ZOO(N)	AIR(T)
ALB(E)	OB(I)	FAD(O)	AMEN(T)
AMID(E)	OBOL(I)	FAR(O)	CHAR(T)
ANIL(E)	SOLD(I)	HOB(O)	ERS(T)

PUT(T)	MEN(U)	NO(W)	FOG(Y)
SKI(T)	TAB(U)	VIE(W)	BE(Z)
EM(U)	CHI(V)	CODE(X)	QUART(Z)
LIE(U)	SO(V)	ALAR(Y)	SPIT(Z)

Setting up Plays

The reason for discussing single-letter prefixing and suffixing at such length is because the experienced Scrabble player not only modifies the words that are already on the board, he puts them there in the first place, so that he can use them subsequently. Good players will often put down a word which they know is capable of being modified by a single letter at the beginning or end. There are two reasons for this. Firstly, it enables certain letters to be counted twice in the scoring process; and secondly, and far more importantly, it gives a potential place to put down a seven-letter word.

Consider the situation in Figure 42. The first player put down the word VYING. The second player, holding GILNORW, used the G of VYING and played GROW. This scored 8 points. He could have played GROWL or GROWN for 10 points, or even GLOW for 8 points. GROW is certainly the best move. He can use his L or N at a subsequent turn (the next turn?), making either GROWL or GROWN, and possibly get down a seven-letter word if he has one. GLOW would have been a pointless play, because the only letter which can be added to its end is S, and he doesn't have one of those. GROWL can only be suffixed with an S (making GROWLS) or a Y (making GROWLY), and he had neither an S nor a Y. GROWN cannot be suffixed at all. The first player follows GROW by playing MUGGY. At this stage, the second player is now holding EGILNRT. With these letters he can make RINGLET, TINGLER and TRINGLE. He now uses the opening that he has created for himself with the word GROW. He could play TRINGLE and GROWN for 69 points, or any of TRINGLE and GROWL, RINGLET and GROWL, RINGLET and

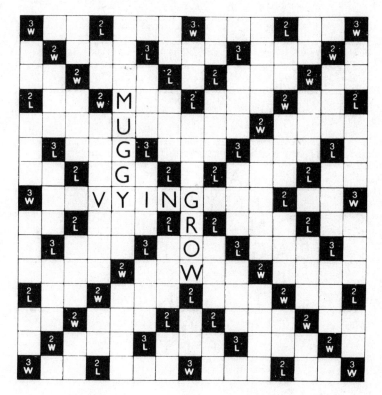

Figure 42

GROWN, TINGLER and GROWL, and TINGLER and GROWN, all scoring 78 points. Had he not played GROW as his first move, he probably wouldn't have had a seven-letter word that went down on the board at his second turn.

When you set up plays like this, you always run the risk that your opponent will do something to wreck your plans. This is why it is much more difficult to get down bonus words in games with three or four players. With three players, you have twice as many opponents as you would have in a two-player game; and with four players, you have three times as many opponents. In three and

Figure 43

four-player games, setting up plays for yourself is considerably less important than it is in two-player games.

Figure 43 illustrates a case where a player has to make an opening. You have the letters EEGILN and a blank on your rack. You can see a host of words on your rack (FEELING, FLEEING, GLEEING, HEELING, JEELING, KEELING, LEERING, REELING and SEELING), but none of them will go down anywhere. What do you do? You have to make an opening, a short word that you will be able to prefix or suffix at your next turn, assuming that you will still be able to make a seven-letter word, and also assuming that your opponent doesn't block the opening you make. There is little point in playing FEE (or FEEL) and EX in the bottom, left-hand corner of the board. This will pull in 21 or 23 points, but does not offer an opening for your next turn. Leave that corner alone, hoping that your opponent might be tempted by it instead of blocking the opening you are about to make. Put the L from your rack to the right of TI, making TIL for 5 points. You may then be able to play TILE at your next move, along with the seven-letter word you are anticipating. In playing TIL, you also realise that it can be suffixed with an L (making TILL), an S (making TILS), and a T (making TILT). If you need to use your blank as an L, S or T, or if you pick up any one of these letters from the pool, you will have even more scope for your seven-letter word.

Setting up Plays is a Gamble

When you set up plays for yourself, you are taking a gamble, the gamble that you are giving up the prospect of some immediate points for many more points a move or two later. What do you lose if it fails? What does your opponent gain if he uses your opening the way you had intended to do? Remember, he may be sitting there with a seven-letter word on his rack, just itching for an opening for it! Take into account your opponent's skill, the different letters that might be used, the chances of your opponent having these letters rather than the pool having them, whether you have opened up a valuable premium square, and, not at all a matter to be dismissed, your opponent's disposition. Some players will suspect that an opponent is setting up an opening and will block it at all costs. Other players, perhaps too generously, will not block such a set-up play, even though they know full well what you are doing. Other players, even more Machiavellian, will not block an opening for just a few points, as they want to use it themselves for a seven-letter word in the next turn or so. They are gambling that they can get down their bonus word before you can get down yours. Perhaps setting up plays is *not* a gamble, more of a finely calculated risk!

Excessive Consonants

The advice given earlier was to keep a balanced rack of letters — low-value letters, no duplicates, and two or three vowels. If you find yourself sitting on a cluster of consonants, though, even single-point ones, start getting rid of them. Exchange them and get some replacement ones from the pool, or play a word with several consonants in it. Here are 50 words that are top-heavy with consonants. You probably have your own favourites.

BRUNT	GLYPH	MHORR	PHON	VELDT
BUMPH	GNAW	MILK	PSHAW	VERB
CHAMP	GRUFF	MYRRH	PSYCH	VETCH
CHIV	HATCH	MYTH	RHOMB	WHORL
CRWTH	HITCH	NATCH	RHUMB	WITCH
DERV	HYMN	NYMPH	SHAFT	WOMB
DITCH	KETCH	OCHRY	SYLPH	XYLOL
DRUNK	KNELT	OWCHE	THAW	YACHT
FILCH	LARCH	PASHM	THICK	ZLOTY
FIRTH	LYME	PHEW	THROB	ZURF

Excessive Vowels

If your rack contains an excess of vowels, either exchange them and get some replacements from the pool, or play a word with several vowels in it. Here are 50 words suffering from a surfeit of vowels.

ADIEU	AKEE	AURA	EERIE	EYRIE
AEON	ALAE	AURAE	EMEU	HOOEY
AERIE	ALEE	AUTO	EOAN	HUIA
AGEE	ANOA	AYRIE	EPEE	IDEA
AGUE	AREA	BEAU	ETUI	ILIA
AIERY	ARIA	COOEE	EUOI	INIA
AJEE	AULA	COOEY	EVOE	IOTA

LIEU	OBOE	OLEO	OURIE	UREA
NOYAU	OGEE	OLIO	ROUE	UVEA
OBEY	OILY	OORIE	URAO	ZOEA

Keeping Track of the Tiles

In a two-player game, by the time that the last tile has been taken from the pool, you should know precisely what letters your opponent holds. Working out whether he has any high-value letters (FHJKQVWXYZ) is fairly easy. Working out which of the other letters he has is merely a question of counting up the letters on the board and your own rack, and then crediting your opponent with the missing ones. Once you know your opponent's letters, you should be able to work out what he is likely to do with them, and therefore how long you can prolong the game. For example, if he has the Q, all the Us are on the board and unusable, and both the blanks have gone, you have all the time in the world. Play out your letters one or two at a time, making the most points you can from them. You will invariably score better by playing them out slowly like this, rather than playing them out in just one or two longer words. Your opponent won't be able to go out with the Q stuck on his rack. Even if your opponent doesn't have the Q, it will still be useful to know that he has something like AAAIOVV. Again, his options are fairly limited, and he is unlikely to be able to go out for three or four turns. On the other hand, if you find your opponent holding something akin to AEILRST and there is a place to put a seven-letter word on the board, block it. If there is more than one place for the word to go, get rid of as many of your tiles as you can for as many points as you can.

Not only should you keep track of the unplayed tiles at the end of a game, you should try to keep a mental note of what's been played during the game. The high-value letters are fairly easy to mentally tick off as they are played, and the same is true of the medium-value letters once you have had a little practice. There is little point in hoping to pick up an M, say, if both of them are already on the board. Keep checking to see what's likely to be left in the pool during the later stages of the game. If 75 tiles have been played and the FFJKVVZ are still to appear, take care! You don't want to pick up all of them. In which case, try playing only a few letters at a time. You don't want to play six letters, select six new ones from the pool and find that you have picked up six high-value letters!

Also, keep track of the rate at which vowels and consonants are being played. Quite often, there is a flood of vowels in the early stages of the game, and this can lead both players into trouble later on when the consonants start to come out in unexpected numbers. The inverse problem occurs, too. A lot of consonants coming out too soon in the game, with relatively few vowels being played, can close up the board, making bonus plays difficult, if not impossible, later on.

End Play

Most games of Scrabble in which the final scores are within 30 points or so of each other are won or lost in the last few moves. Don't forget that when a player has used all of his tiles and the pool is exhausted, the scores of the other players are reduced by the sum of the point values of the tiles held by each player, and the score of the player who has gone out is increased by the sum of the point values of all the tiles held by his opponents. So, if a game is close towards the end, it is important that you try to go out before your opponents. Going out first in a game with three or four players is even more important than going out first in a game with just one other player. You are likely to pick up two or three times as many points from your opponents than you would in a two-player game. So, when you are near the end of a game, what can you do to improve your own score as best you can and to reduce your opponent's by as many points as possible? First of all, try to get rid of your high-value and medium-value tiles. Don't get stuck with them if you can avoid it, or else your opponent will go out first and your score will suffer from the effects of the letters left on your rack.

Either put those letters down on the board somewhere, or, if that isn't possible, put them back into the pool of unused letters and get some replacements. Suppose there are just three letters left in the pool and on your rack are AEFIQSV. Work out what the 10 outstanding tiles are (the seven on your opponent's rack plus the three in the pool), just to make sure that there are no nasty surprises in store for you (like two Ws and a Z in the pool). Then, exchange the FQV. In this way, you will give your opponent at least one awkward letter, or maybe even all three of them. Let the letters cause him some problems. Make the letters work for you, even if it's only by being left on your opponent's rack at the end of the game. Of course, if you do put back three tiles, you could get one or two of them back. You have put back FQV and picked up EEE, say; your opponent plays one letter, and picks up the Q, say; you play a letter, and then pick up the F; and your opponent plays one letter, and picks up the final V. You have at least managed to dump two of your three unwanted letters onto your opponent. One thing: don't be timid about exchanging right at the end of the game. Your opponent would probably do it to you given half the chance; and if he wouldn't do it to you, he deserves to have it done to him, anyway!

If you decide to return awkward letters to the pool near the end of the game, be careful not to put them back too soon. The more tiles you return and the sooner you do it, the greater are your chances of getting them back again.

If you decide against exchanging any letters at the end of a game, you must make your end-game plays the best possible, and these are not necessarily the ones scoring the most points. Consider this example. You have EFGGOYZ on your rack, and your opponent has just one letter on his. He is almost certain to go out on his next turn. You might be able to make EGGY and some other words for a total of 30 points, or FOZY for only 21 points. But FOZY is the better move. Why? If your opponent goes out on his next turn, he will catch you holding EGG (worth 5 points). That's five points added to his score, and five points deducted from your score. This means that you have made a net score of 11 points.

(That is, 21 points minus 5 points twice.) But had you played EGGY for 30 points, and then your opponent had gone out, he would catch you for 15 points, with FOZ on your rack. He will get 15 points added to his score, and you will get 15 points deducted from yours. The net value to you is zero points. (That is, 30 points minus 15 points twice.) Thus, FOZY is worth 11 points more to you than EGGY, even though it actually scores 9 points *less* when it is played!

Summary

Scrabble players are basically of two types, defensive and offensive. How a particular game turns out will depend on your personality, that of your opponent, and what each of you perceives the object of the game to be. Is it to win? Is it to win and score highly? Is it to score highly? If winning is all-important, a player may be quite happy to finish with 250 points against his opponent's 240 points. If you want to score highly as well, you may be dissatisfied with any win that doesn't score at least 450 points. A win of 500 points to 400 will please you; a win of 410 to 400 won't please you. Other players have another objective, merely to enjoy the game! But the very best players somehow manage to optimise all three objectives. They win, they score highly, and they enjoy the game.

If you aim only to win, regardless of what the final scores are, your best bet is a defensive game. In such a game, players tend to use lots of short words and lots of tightly interlocking words. They open up very little of the board, hoping to stop their opponent from scoring highly. If the opponent attempts to make an opening for himself, that is likely to be blocked quickly. A defensive player will avoid opening up the more valuable premium squares. However, while a defensive player is trying to make life difficult for his opponent, he must try to avoid giving himself a hard time. This is where many inexperienced defensive players go wrong. They often end up with exactly the same problems that their opponent has. Good defensive play is an art, just as is good offensive play. But it can be more easily achieved and is usually less elegant than good

Figure 44

offensive play. The words played in a defensive type of game are often clustered in just one half of the board, any opportunity of using the other half of the board having been largely eliminated. Figure 44 is an example of a partly finished defensive game. There is only a slim chance of this game expanding to the other half of the board. Many inexperienced players find themselves in this situation quite by accident, having successfully managed to thwart their opponent's play as well as their own! It takes a good player to get the best from such tight situations.

Figure 45

An offensive player goes all out for 50-point bonuses. He runs risks, and he opens up premium score squares, especially triple-word-score squares, for his opponent, in the hope that the board will quickly be opened up even further, giving him plenty of opportunities to get his bonus words down. Good offensive play tends to be quite elegant. A good player will hop about the board, using a premium square here, opening up a premium square there, and collecting four or five bonuses in the process. The bonuses will have sandwiched between them quite a few intermediate scores, in the 25-40 points range. Of course, an offensive player doesn't just open up any old premium squares for his opponent. There will be times when he just cannot afford to do this. If he knows that his opponent has a blank on his rack, there is no point in handing him a place to put his bonus word that gets tripled in the process.

If an opponent is not an accomplished player, he may be unable to take advantage of the premium squares offered him, so the 'carrots' being dangled in front of him are wasted, but they can then be used by the more experienced player. On the other hand, two very experienced players, both fully aware of each other's vocabulary, style, temperament, and capabilities will often play a lot less offensively against each other than they would do against lesser players. They know only too well that any premium squares opened up are likely to be promptly and effectively used, but with no new premium squares being opened up as a result. Figure 45 illustrates a particularly open and high-scoring game, the product of some good offensive play. (The letters EK remained unplayed at the end of the game, and the blanks were used as the U of CONQUERS and the T of BARONETS.)

Scrabble Records

Scrabble players are always enquiring what the highest possible score for a single move is. Or what the highest actual score for a complete game is. Or how long was the longest game. And so on. A number of Scrabble records are described here. If you can beat any of them, or you have a different kind of record, please send the *full* details to me:

> Gyles Brandreth
> c/o Robert Hale Ltd
> Clerkenwell House
> 45-47 Clerkenwell Green
> London EC1R 0HT

Here are the records.

Highest Score on the First Move
The highest theoretical scores, with different numbers of letters, that can be achieved on the very first move in a game are as follows:

2 letters – ZO (22 points). This is in Chambers.

3 letters – ZAX (38 points). This is in Chambers.

4 letters – QUIZ (48 points). This is in Chambers.

5 letters – SQUIZ (66 points). This is *not* in Chambers. It means a glance or a look, and can be found in *Webster's Third New International Dictionary*. The highest-scoring words from Chambers are JAZZY, QUAKY, ZANJA, ZINKY, ZIPPY and ZYMIC, all being worth 62 points. Note that it is necessary to use a blank as a Z in JAZZY.

6 letters – QUEAZY (74 points). This is in Chambers.

7 letters – ZYXOMMA (130 points). This is *not* in Chambers. It is a type of Indian dragonfly, and can be found in Funk and Wagnall's *New Standard Dictionary*. The highest-scoring word from Chambers is QUARTZY, worth 126 points.

Highest Score for First Two Moves
The highest theoretical score that can be achieved on the first two moves of a game is 314 points. The first player puts down HYDROXY for 102 points, with the second Y on the centre square. This word is *not* in Chambers, but is in the 1979 edition of *Collins English Dictionary*. The second player turns the first word into HYDROXYBENZOIC, scoring 212 points. This is *not* in Chambers, but is in the 1972 Supplement to the *Oxford English Dictionary*. The two scores added together come to 314 points.

Highest Real Score in a Single Move
The highest known score achieved at a single move in a real game is 374 points. This was achieved by playing the word QUETZALS

across two triple-word-score squares, and getting the Z on a double-letter-score square. This score was made by Darryl Francis, of Wandsworth, London, on 12th September 1973.

Highest Real Game Score
The highest known score achieved by one player in a real game is 730 points. This was achieved by Ron Hendra, of Wimbledon, London, on 12th July 1978. His opponent's score for the game was 360 points.

Most Bonuses in a Real Game
The highest number of 50-point bonuses in a real game is 7. This was achieved by Darryl Francis, of Wandsworth, London, on 9th March 1974. Mr Francis' total score at the end of the game was 656 points.

Highest Idealised Score in a Single Move
In an idealised game, the highest score yet discovered for *one single move* is 1961 points. This idealised move was devised by Ron Jerome, of Bracknell, Berkshire, in May 1974. The move involved playing all seven tiles, combining them with eight already on the board, to form a 15-letter word, which stretched across three triple-word-score squares. As well as making this 15-letter word, the move also created seven words perpendicular to it, three of them stretching across triple-word-score squares.

The 15-letter word that was played was BENZOXYCAMPHORS. The seven other words were DAFFODILLY, GULLISH, JINNYRICKSHAWS, PROVERB, SQUANDERMANIAC, VAGABONDAGER, and WERTUZ. (The words DAFFODILL, GULLIS, JINNYRICKSHAW, PROVER, SQUANDERMANIA, VAGABONDAGE, and WERTU were already on the board.)

Where can all these strange words be found?

BENZOXYCAMPHORS – *Webster's New International Dictionary*, Second edition
DAFFODILL – *Oxford English Dictionary*
DAFFODILLY – Chambers
GULLIS – *Oxford English Dictionary*
GULLISH – Chambers
JINNYRICKSHAW(S) – *Oxford English Dictionary*
PROVER – Chambers
PROVERB – Chambers
SQUANDERMANIA – Chambers
SQUANDERMANIAC – *Webster's New International Dictionary*, Second Edition
VAGABONDAGE – Chambers
VAGABONDAGER – *Oxford English Dictionary*
WERTU – *Oxford English Dictionary*
WERTUZ – *Oxford English Dictionary*

Highest Idealised Game Score
In an idealised game, the highest final score for one player that has yet been discovered is 4153 points. This idealised game was devised by Ralph Beaman, of Pennsylvania, USA, in 1974.

Longest Game
The longest game lasted 120 hours. This was achieved by Norman Hazeldean, Alan Giles, Tom Barton, and Keith Ollett, at Uckfield, East Sussex, from 4th to 9th August 1975.

Most British National Championships
The only person to have the British National Championships twice is Olive Behan, of Widnes, Lancashire. She won the championship in 1972 and 1975.

4
Scrabble Vocabulary

The essential lists of words that will enable a Scrabble player to become a true master of the game. Every word listed will be allowed at the National Scrabble Championship.

Two-letter Words

This is a complete list of the two-letter words which are allowable under the rules of the National Scrabble Championship from 1980 onwards. All 86 of the words are in *Chambers Twentieth Century Dictionary* (with 1977 Supplement).

Next to each word is (i) an abbreviation indicating the word's part of speech (adj = adjective, adv = adverb, int = interjection, n = noun, prep = preposition, pron = pronoun, and vb = verb), and (ii) a brief meaning for the word.

Where a word has more than one part of speech, only the most useful one is indicated. For example, IF is shown in Chambers as a noun as well as a conjunction; because the noun allows for the addition of an S at the end, but the conjunction doesn't, the noun part of speech and meaning are given. There are similar examples: EH is more useful as a verb than an interjection, HE is more useful as a noun than as a pronoun, and SO is more useful as a noun than as an adverb or conjunction.

Meanings are given to help the reader fix a word in his mind. It is usually the case that a word is more easily remembered if it has some meaning associated with it. It is then no mere sequence of letters.

Word	Part of speech	Meaning
AD	n	colloquial for 'advertisement'
AE	adj	Scots form of 'one'
AH	int	expressing joy, pity, surprise, etc
AI	n	the three-toed sloth
AM	vb	first person singular of the verb 'to be'
AN	adj	an indefinite article
AS	adv	in whatever manner
AT	prep	denoting position
AX	vb	to cut down
AY	adv	yes
BE	vb	to exist
BO	int	used to frighten children
BY	prep	near to
DA	n	a Burmese knife
DO	vb	to perform
EA	n	a river
EE	n	Scots form of 'eye'
EH	vb	to say the interjection 'eh'
EL	n	anything of the shape of the letter L
EM	n	a unit of measurement used in printing
EN	n	half an em
ER	int	expressing hesitation
ES	n	anything of the shape of the letter S
EX	n	one who is no longer what he was
FA	n	a musical note
FY	int	denoting disgust
GO	vb	to proceed
GU	n	a kind of violin
HA	int	denoting grief, joy, surprise, etc
HE	n	a male
HI	int	calling attention
HO	n	cessation
ID	n	a fish

IF	n	a condition
IN	vb	to gather in harvest
IO	n	a cry of grief, joy or triumph
IS	vb	part of the verb 'to be'
IT	pron	the neuter form of 'he' and 'him'
JO	n	a beloved one
KA	n	genius
KY	n	cows
LA	n	a musical note
LI	n	a Chinese unit of distance
LO	int	behold!
MA	n	a childish contraction of 'mamma'
ME	n	a musical note
MI	n	a musical note
MO	adj	more
MY	int	expressing surprise
NA	adv	Scots form of 'no'
NO	n	Japanese drama
OB	n	an objection
OD	n	a type of force
OE	n	a grandchild
OF	prep	belonging to
OH	int	denoting pain, sorrow, surprise, etc
ON	vb	to go on
OO	pron	Scots form of 'we'
OR	n	the tincture gold
OU	int	expressing concession
OW	int	expressing concession
OX	n	the common domestic cattle
OY	n	a grandchild
PA	n	a childish word for 'father'
PI	n	a mixed state
RE	n	a musical note
SH	int	hush
SI	n	a musical note
SO	n	a musical note

ST	int	hush
TA	int	thank you
TE	n	a musical note
TI	n	a musical note
TO	adv	in the direction of
UG	vb	to excite loathing in
UN	pron	one
UP	vb	to drive up-stream
UR	int	filling a gap in speech
US	pron	the objective case of 'we'
UT	n	a musical note
WE	pron	the plural of 'I'
WO	n	a calamity
YE	pron	you
YO	int	calling for effort
YU	n	a precious jade
ZO	n	a hybrid domestic cattle of the Himalayas

Three-letter Words

This is a complete list of the three-letter words which are allowable under the rules of the National Scrabble Championship from 1980 onwards. All the words are in *Chambers Twentieth Century Dictionary* (with 1977 Supplement) or are plural or verb forms (created by the addition of an S) of two-letter words in the dictionary.

The words have been split into four groups. Group I is composed of words where the first two letters and the last two letters of each word are both themselves two-letter words (for example, ADO is composed of both AD and DO); group II is composed of words where only the last two letters of each word form a two-letter word (for example, AGO has only its last two letters making a word, GO; AG is not an allowable two-letter word); group III is composed of words where only the first two letters of each word form a two-letter word (for example, ADD has only its first two letters making a word, AD; DD is not, of course, an allowable two-letter word); and group IV is composed of words where neither the first two letters nor the last two letters of each word form a two-letter word (for example, in the word ACE, neither AC nor CE is an allowable two-letter word).

Some of the words in these four lists are not easy to locate in the dictionary. Where it seems helpful to give the reader guidance as to a word's precise location, a number appears to the right of the word; and at the end of each group of words is a list of numbers and where the associated words can be found in the dictionary. For example, KOW is not shown anywhere in the K section of the dictionary; it can only be found at COW. Another example is PYE, which can only be found at PIE.

STOP PRESS. Since these lists were originally compiled we have completed the 1980 National Scrabble Championships and a few more words are now regarded as permissible. They include: AHS, ANE, AYS, BOS, BYS, FYS, GAE, GIF, GOS, GUS, HUM, ICH, JOS KYE, MUX, MYS, NOY, OHS, OOR, OUS, OWS, SHS, SIM, SOV, TAS, TAU, ULT, UNS, URS, VAC, VIA, VIZ, VOX, WAE, WOS, YOS.

Group I

ADO	BEE	BOY	DOH
AHA	BEL	BYE	DON
AID	BEN	DAD	DOO
AIN	BOB	DAH[3]	DOR
AIS[1]	BOD	DAM	DOW
AIT	BOH[2]	DAN	EAS[5]
ANA	BOO	DAS[4]	EAT
ASH	BOR	DAY	EEL
ATE	BOW	DOD	EEN[6]
AYE	BOX	DOE	ERE

115

FAD	ION	MID	REE
FAH	ISH	MIS[15]	REH
FAN	ITA	MOB	REM
FAS[7]	JOB	MOD	REN[18]
FAT	JOE	MOO	RES[19]
FAY	JOW	MOR[16]	SHE
GOB	JOY	MOU	SIN
GOD	KAE	MOW	SIS[20]
GOE	KAS[9]	NAE	SIT
GOO	KAT	NAM	SOB
GOY	KAY[10]	NAY	SOD
GUN	KYE	NOB	SOH
GUP	LAD	NOD	SON
GUR	LAH	NOH	SOU
GUT	LAM	NOR	SOW
HAD	LAS[11]	NOW	SOX
HAE	LAT	OES[17]	SOY
HAH	LAX	OHO	TAE
HAM	LAY	OOF	TAI
HAS	LID	OON	TAM
HAT	LIN	ORE	TAN
HAY	LIS	OUP	TAT
HEM	LIT	OUR	TAX
HEN	LOB	OUT	TEA
HER	LOO	OWE	TEE
HES[8]	LOW	OYE	TEL
HEX	LOX	PAD	TEN
HID	LOY	PAH	TES[21]
HIN	MAD	PAM	TID
HIS	MAE[12]	PAN	TIN
HIT	MAN	PAS	TIS[22]
HOB	MAS[13]	PAT	TIT
HOD	MAT	PAX	TOD
HOE	MAY	PAY	TOE
HOW	MEN	PIN	TON
HOY	MES[14]	PIT	TOO

116

TOR	WEN	YEN	YOW
TOW	WOE	YES	YUG
TOY	WON	YEX	YUS[23]
URE	WOO	YOB	ZOO[24]
WEE	WOW	YON	
WEM	YEA	YOU	

1. plural of AI   2. see BO   3. see DA   4. plural of DA
5. plural of EA   6. see EE   7. plural of FA   8. see HE
9. plural of KA   10. see QUAY   11. plural of LA   12. see 1st MO
13. plural of MA   14. plural of ME   15. plural of MI   16. see MAUTHER
17. plural of OE   18. see RUN   19. plural of RE   20. plural of SI
21. plural of TE   22. plural of TI   23. plural of YU   24. see ZOO-

Group II

ABY	BUR	COX	EWE
AGO	BUS	COY	EYE
ALA	BUT	CUP	FEE
ARE	CAD	CUR	FEN
AWE	CAM	CUT	FID
BAD	CAN	DEE	FIN
BAH	CAT	DEN	FIT
BAM	CAY	DID	FOB
BAN	CHA	DIN	FOE
BAT	CHI	DIT	FOH
BAY	CIT	DSO	FOR
BID	COB	DUG	FOU
BIN	COD	DUN	FOX
BIS	CON	DYE	FOY
BIT	COO	DZO	FUG
BUG	COR	EGO	FUN
BUN	COW	EON	FUR

GAD	LEE	RAN	TUG
GAE	LUG	RAS	TUN
GAM	LUR	RAT	TUP
GAN	LYE	RAX	TUT
GAS	MHO	RAY	TWO
GAT	MNA	RID	TYE
GAY	MUG	RIN	UDO
GEE	MUN	RIT	VAE
GEL	NID	ROB	VAN
GEM	NIS	ROD	VAS
GEN	NIT	ROE	VAT
GHI	NUN	ROW	VEE
GID	NUR	RUG	VEX
GIN	NUT	RUN	VOE
GIO	OAT	RUT	VOW
HUG	PEA	RYE	VUG
HUP	PEE	SAD	WAD
HUT	PEN	SAE	WAN
IRE	PER	SAI	WAS
JAM	PHO	SAT	WAT
JAY	POD	SAX	WAX
JEE	POH	SAY	WAY
JUG	POW	SEA	WHO
JUT	POX	SEE	WIN
KEA	PUG	SEL	WIS
KEN	PUN	SEN	WIT
KEX	PUP	SEX	WYE
KID	PUR	SKY	YAH
KIN	PUS	SPA	YAM
KIT	PUT	SUN	YIN
KOB	PYE[2]	SUP	ZAX
KOW[1]	RAD	SYE	ZEL
LEA	RAM	THE	ZHO

1. see 2nd COW   2. see 2nd PIE

Group III

ADD	EAR	HEW	LOS
ADS[1]	EAU	HEY	LOT
AIA	EHS[3]	HIC	MAC[11]
AIL	ELD	HIE	MAG
AIM	ELF	HIM	MAK
AIR	ELK	HIP	MAP
AMP	ELL	HOA	MAR
AND	ELM	HOG	MAW
ANN	ELS[4]	HOP	MET
ANT	ELT	HOS[6]	MEU
ANY	EMS[5]	HOT	MEW
ASK	EMU	IDE	MIL
ASP	END	IDS[7]	MIM
ASS	ENE	IFS[8]	MIR
AXE	ENS	INK	MIX
BED	ERA	INN	MOA
BEG	ERG	INS[9]	MOG[12]
BET	ERK	ISM	MOP
BEY	ERR	ITS	NAB
BEZ	ERS	JOG	NAG
BOA	ESS	JOT	NAP
BOG	FAB	KAW[10]	NOG
BOP	FAG	LAB	NOT
BOT	FAR	LAC	OBI
DAB	FAW	LAG	OBS[13]
DAG	GOT	LAP	ODD
DAK	GUE	LAR	ODE
DAL	GUM	LAW	ODS[14]
DAP	GUY	LIB	OFF
DAW	HAG	LIE	OFT
DOG	HAP	LIG	OHM
DOP	HAW	LIP	ONE
DOS[2]	HEP	LOG	ONS[15]
DOT	HET	LOP	OOP

ORB	RET	TAK	UGH
ORC	REV	TAP	UGS[19]
ORS[16]	SHY	TAR	UPS[20]
ORT	SIB	TAU	URN
OUK	SIC	TAW	USE
OWL	SIP	TED	UTS[21]
OWN	SIR	TEF	WEB
OYS[17]	SIX	TEG	WED
PAL	SOC	TEW	WET
PAP	SOG	TIC	WEY
PAR	SOL	TIE	WOG
PAW	SOP	TIG	WOP
PIA	SOS[18]	TIL	WOT
PIE	SOT	TIP	YET
PIG	STY	TOG	YEW
PIP	TAB	TOM	YUK[22]
PIX	TAG	TOP	ZOA[23]
RED	TAJ	TOT	ZOS[24]
REP			

1. plural of AD   2. plural of DO   3. form of verb EH   4. plural of EL
5. plural of EM   6. plural of HO   7. plural of ID   8. plural of IF
9. form of verb IN   10. see CAW   11. see MACKINTOSH   12. see MOGGY
13. plural of OB   14. plural of OD   15. form of verb ON   16. plural of OR
17. plural of OY   18. plural of SO   19. form of verb UG   20. form of verb UP
21. plural of UT   22. see 1977 Supplement   23. plural of ZOON, see ZOO-
24. plural of ZO

Group IV

ABA	BRA	DUE	GAL
ABB	BUB	DUO	GAP
ACE	BUD	DUX	GAR
ACT	BUM	EBB	GAU
AFT	BUY	ECU	GED
AGA	CAB	EFT	GEO
AGE	CAP	EGG	GET
AKE	CAR	EIK	GEY
ALB	CAW	EKE	GIB
ALE	CIG[1]	EUK	GIE
ALL	CLY	EVE	GIG
ALP	COG	EWK[2]	GIP
ALS	COL	EWT	GJU
ALT	COP	FED	GNU
APE	COS	FEU	GYP
APT	COT	FEW	HUB
ARC	COZ	FEY	HUE
ARK	CRY	FEZ	HYP
ARM	CUB	FIB	ICE
ART	CUD	FIE	ICY[4]
ARY	CUE	FIG	ILK
AUF	CUM	FIR	ILL
AUK	DEB	FIX	IMP
AVA	DEW	FIZ[3]	IRK
AVE	DEY	FLU	IVY
AWL	DIB	FLY	JAB
AWN	DIE	FOG	JAG
BAA	DIG	FOP	JAK
BAG	DIM	FRY	JAP
BAP	DIP	FUB	JAR
BAR	DIV	FUD	JAW
BIB	DRY	FUM	JET
BIG	DUB	GAB	JIB
BIZ	DUD	GAG	JIG

JIZ	NIM	RAJ	SUD[5]
JUD	NIP	RAP	SUE
KEB	NIX	RAW	SUM
KED	NUB	RIA	THY
KEF	OAF	RIB	TRY
KEG	OAK	RIG	TUB
KEP	OAR	RIM	TUI
KET	OCA	RIP	TUM
KEY	OCH	ROC	TWA
KIP	OIL	ROK	UDS
KOA	OKE	ROM	ULE
KOS	OLD	ROT	UVA
LED	OPE	RUB	VET
LEG	OPT	RUC	VIE
LEI	OVA	RUD	VIM
LEP	PEC	RUE	VOL
LET	PED	RUM	WAG
LEU	PEG	SAB	WAP
LEV	PEP	SAC	WAR
LEW	PET	SAG	WAW
LEY	PEW	SAL	WHY
LUD	PLY	SAP	WIG
LUM	POI	SAR	WRY
LUX	POM	SAW	WUD
LUZ	POP	SEC	YAK
MUD	POT	SEG	YAP
MUM	PRO	SET	YAW
NEB	PRY	SEW	YIP
NEF	PUB	SEY	ZAP[6]
NEP	PUD	SEZ	ZED
NET	PUY	SKI	ZIP
NEW	PYX	SLY	ZUZ
NIB	QUA	SPY	
NIL	RAG	SUB	

1. see CIGAR   2. see YUKE   3. see FIZZ   4. see ICE
5. see SUDS   6. see 1977 Supplement

122

Four-letter and Five-letter Words with High-value Letters

This is a list of four-letter and five-letter words having a J, Q, X or Z, and which are allowable under the rules of the National Scrabble Championship from 1980 onwards. All the words are in *Chambers Twentieth Century Dictionary* (with 1977 Supplement).

Generally, plurals and verb forms of two-, three- and four-letter words have been omitted from these lists.

As with the three-letter words, some of these words are not easy to locate in the dictionary. Where it seems helpful to give the reader guidance as to a word's precise location, a number appears to the right of the word. At the end of the four-letter list is a list of numbers and where the associated words can be found in the dictionary. A similar list of numbers and locations follows the list of five-letter words.

Four-letter Words with High-value Letters

J

AJAR	JANN	JEER	JINK
AJEE	JAPE	JEFF	JINN
BENJ	JARK	JELL[2]	JINX
GAJO	JARL	JERK	JIVE
HADJ	JASY[1]	JESS	JOBE[3]
HAJJ	JATO	JEST	JOCO
JACK	JAUP	JETE	JOEY[4]
JADE	JAZY	JIBE	JOIN
JAIL	JAZZ	JIFF	JOKE
JAKE	JEAN	JILL	JOLE
JAMB	JEEL	JILT	JOLL[5]
JANE	JEEP	JIMP	JOLT

Q

JOMO	JUMP	QUAD
JOOK[6]	JUNK	QUAG
JOSH	JURY	QUAT
JOSS	JUST	QUAY
JOTA	JUTE	QUEY
JOUK	PUJA	QUID
JOWL	RAJA[7]	QUIN
JUBA	SOJA	QUIP
JUBE		QUIT
JUDO		QUIZ
JUDY		QUOD
JUKE		QUOP

X   **Z**

APEX	FLEX	PREX	ADZE
AXED[8]	FLIX	ROUX	AZYM
AXES	FLUX	SEXT	BUZZ
AXIL[9]	FOXY[13]	SEXY[19]	CHEZ
AXIS	HOAX	TAXA[20]	COZE
AXLE	IBEX	TAXI	COZY
AXON	ILEX	TEXT	CZAR
CALX	IYNX	WAXY[21]	DAZE
COAX	JINX	XYST[22]	DOZE
COXA	LANX	YUNX	DOZY[23]
COXY	LYNX		FIZZ
CRUX	MINX		FOZY
DIXY[10]	MIXT[14]		FRIZ[24]
DOXY	MIXY[15]		FUZE
EXAM[11]	MOXA		FUZZ
EXIT	NEXT		GAZE
EXON	NIXY[16]		GAZY[25]
EXPO[12]	ONYX		GIZZ
FAIX	OXEN[17]		HAZE
FALX	OXER[18]		HAZY[26]
FLAX	PIXY		JAZY

124

JAZZ	PIZE	ZARF	ZOBU
LAZE[27]	QUIZ	ZATI	ZOEA
LAZY	RAZE	ZEAL	ZOIC
MAZE	RAZZ	ZEBU	ZONA
MAZY[28]	SIZE	ZEIN	ZONE
MOZE	SWIZ	ZERO	ZOOM
NAZE	TOZE	ZEST	ZOON[30]
OOZE	TUZZ	ZETA	ZUPA
OOZY[29]	TZAR	ZILA	ZURF
OUZO	VIZY	ZIMB	ZYME
OYEZ	WHIZ	ZINC	
PHIZ	ZANY	ZOBO	

1. see JASEY 2. see JELLY 3. see 1st JOB 4. see 1st JOE
5. see JOLE 6. see JOUK 7. see RAJ 8. form of verb AXE
9. see AXILLA 10. see DIXIE 11. see EXAMINE 12. see 1977 Supplement
13. see FOX 14. see MIX 15. see MIX 16. see 1st NIX
17. see OX 18. see OX 19. see SEX 20. see TAXIS
21. see 1st and 3rd WAX 22. see XYSTUS 23. see DOZE 24. see FRIZZ
25. see GAZE 26. see HAZE 27. see LAZY 28. see MAZE
29. see OOZE 30. see ZOO-

Five-letter Words with High-value Letters

J

AJWAN	JANTY	JINNI[15]	JUMPY[21]
BAJAN	JAPAN	JINNS[16]	JUNCO
BAJRA	JARTA	JOCKO	JUNTA
BAJRI	JARUL	JODEL	JUNTO[22]
BANJO	JASEY	JOINT	JUPON
BIJOU	JASPE[9]	JOIST	JURAL
DJINN	JAUNT	JOKER[17]	JURAT
ENJOY	JAWAN	JOLLY	JUROR[23]
FJORD	JAWED[10]	JONTY	JUTTY
GANJA	JAZZY[11]	JORAM[18]	KHOJA
HADJI[1]	JEELY	JORUM	KOPJE
HAJJI[2]	JEHAD	JOTUN	MAJOR
HEJRA	JELLY	JOUGS	MUJIK
HIJRA	JEMMY	JOULE	OUIJA
HODJA[3]	JERID	JOUST	POOJA
JABOT	JERKY[12]	JOWAR	RAJAH[24]
JADED[4]	JERRY	JOYED[19]	SAJOU
JAGER	JETON[13]	JUDAS	SHOJI
JAGGY[5]	JETTY	JUDGE	UPJET
JAGIR[6]	JEWEL	JUGAL	YOJAN
JALAP	JIFFY	JUICE	ZANJA
JAMBE[7]	JIGOT	JUICY[20]	
JAMBU	JIHAD	JULEP	
JAMES	JIMPY[14]	JUMBO	
JAMMY[8]	JINGO	JUMBY	

Q

EQUAL	QUACK	QUAKY[25]	QUART
EQUIP	QUAFF	QUALM	QUASH
MAQUI	QUAIL	QUANT	QUASI
PIQUE	QUAKE	QUARK	QUEAN

QUEEN	QUIFF	QUIRT	SQUAB
QUEER	QUILL	QUIST	SQUAD
QUELL	QUILT	QUITE	SQUAT
QUERN	QUINA	QUOIF	SQUAW
QUERY	QUINE	QUOIN	SQUIB
QUEST	QUINT	QUOIT	SQUID
QUEUE	QUIPO[27]	QUOTA	SQUIT
QUEYN[26]	QUIPU	QUOTE	TOQUE
QUICK	QUIRE	QUOTH	TUQUE
QUIET	QUIRK	ROQUE[28]	

X

ADDAX	DIXIE	HELIX	PODEX
ADMIX	DRUXY	HEXAD[39]	PREXY[49]
AFFIX	EMBOX	INDEX	PROXY
ANNEX	EPOXY	INFIX	PYXIS[50]
ATAXY	EXACT	IXTLE	RADIX
AUXIN	EXALT	KYLIX	RELAX
AXIAL	EXCEL	LATEX	REMEX
AXILE	EXEAT	LAXLY[40]	SEXED[51]
AXIOM	EXERT	LUXES[41]	SILEX
AXOID[29]	EXIES	MALAX	SIXER[52]
BEAUX[30]	EXILE	MAXIM	SIXTE[53]
BORAX	EXINE	MIXED[42]	SIXTH[54]
BOXEN[31]	EXIST	MIXEN	SIXTY
BOXER[32]	EXODE	MIXER[43]	TAXED[55]
BRAXY	EXPEL	NEXUS	TAXER[56]
BUXOM	EXTOL	NIXIE[44]	TAXIS
CALIX	EXTRA	NOXAL[45]	TAXON[57]
CALYX	EXUDE	OXEYE[46]	TAXOR[58]
CAXON	EXULT	OXIDE	TELEX
CHOUX[33]	FIXED[35]	OXLIP	TEXAS
CODEX	FIXER[36]	OXTER	TOXIC
COXAL[34]	FLAXY[37]	PIXEL[47]	TOXIN[59]
CYLIX	FOXED[38]	PIXIE[48]	UNFIX

127

UNSEX   VIBEX   XENIA[64]   XYLOL[68]
UNTAX   VIXEN   XENON[65]   XYLYL[69]
VARIX   WAXEN[62]   XERIC[66]
VEXED[60]   WAXER[63]   XYLEM
VEXER[61]   XEBEC   XYLIC[67]

Z

ABUZZ	DIZZY	HUZZA	ROZET
AGAZE	DOZED[78]	HUZZY	ROZIT
AMAZE	DOZEN	IZARD	SARZA[96]
AZOIC	DOZER[79]	JAZZY[90]	SEIZE
AZOTE	FEEZE	KAZOO	SENZA
AZOTH	FEZES[80]	KUDZU	SIZAR[97]
AZURY[70]	FIZZY[81]	LAZAR	SIZED[98]
AZYGY[71]	FRIZZ	LEAZE	SIZEL
AZYME[72]	FROZE[82]	LOZEN[91]	SIZER[99]
BAIZE	FURZE	MAIZE	SPITZ
BAZAR	FURZY[83]	MATZA[92]	TAZZA
BEZEL	FUZEE[84]	MATZO	TAZZE
BLAZE	FUZZY[85]	MAZER	TIZZY
BLITZ	GAUZE	MAZUT	TOPAZ
BONZE	GAUZY[86]	MIZEN[93]	TOUZE
BOOZE	GAZAL[87]	MUZZY	TOWZE
BOOZY[73]	GAZEL	NAZIR	TOZIE
BRAZE	GAZER[88]	NEEZE	UNZIP
BUAZE	GAZON	NIZAM	VEZIR
BUZZY[74]	GHAZI	NIZAR	VIZIR[100]
BWAZI[75]	GLAZE	OUZEL	VIZOR
COLZA	GLOZE	OZONE	WALTZ
COZEN	GRAZE	PIEZO[94]	WAZIR
CRAZE	GRIZE	PLAZA	WEIZE
CRAZY[76]	HAZEL	PRIZE	WHIZZ
CROZE	HAZER[89]	RAZED[95]	WINZE
DARZI	HEEZE	RAZEE	WIZEN
DAZED[77]	HERTZ	RAZOR	WOOTZ
		RITZY	

WOOZY	ZIBET	ZOEAE[106]	ZOOKS
ZABRA	ZIGAN	ZOEAL[107]	ZOPPO
ZAMBO	ZIMBI	ZOISM	ZORIL
ZANJA	ZINCO[102]	ZOIST[108]	ZORRO
ZANTE	ZINCY[103]	ZOMBI	ZUPAN[114]
ZANZE	ZINKE	ZONAE[109]	ZYGAL[115]
ZEBEC	ZINKY[104]	ZONAL[110]	ZYGON[116]
ZEBRA	ZIPPY[105]	ZONDA	ZYMIC[117]
ZEBUB	ZIZEL	ZONED[111]	
ZERDA	ZLOTY	ZOOEA[112]	
ZHOMO[101]	ZOCCO	ZOOID[113]	

1. see HADJ   2. see HADJ   3. see KHOJA   4. see 1st JADE
5. see 1st JAG   6. see JAGHIR   7. see JAMB   8. see 1st JAM
9. see JASP   10. see 1st JAW   11. see JAZZ   12. see 1st and 3rd JERK
13. see JETTON   14. see JIMP   15. see JINN   16. see JINN
17. see JOKE   18. see JORUM   19. see JOY   20. see JUICE
21. see 1st JUMP   22. see JUNTA   23. see JURY   24. see RAJ
25. see QUAKE   26. see QUEAN   27. see QUIPU   28. see ROQUET
29. see AXIS   30. see 1st BEAU   31. see 1st BOX   32. see 3rd BOX
33. see CHOU   34. see COXA   35. see FIX   36. see FIX
37. see FLAX   38. see FOX   39. see HEX-   40. see LAX
41. see LUX   42. see MIX   43. see MIX   44. see 1st NIX
45. see NOXIOUS   46. see OX   47. see 1977 Supplement   48. see PIXY
49. see PREX   50. see PYX   51. see SEX   52. see SIX
53. see SIXAINE   54. see SIX   55. see TAX   56. see TAX
57. see TAXIS   58. see TAX   59. see TOXIC   60. see VEX
61. see VEX   62. see 1st and 2nd WAX   63. see 1st WAX   64. see XEN-
65. see XEN-   66. see XER-   67. see XYLEM   68. see XYLEM
69. see XYLEM   70. see AZURE   71. see AZYGOUS   72. see AZYM
73. see BOOZE   74. see 1st BUZZ   75. see BUAZE   76. see CRAZE
77. see DAZE   78. see DOZE   79. see DOZE   80. see FEZ
81. see FIZ   82. see FREEZE   83. see FURZE   84. see 1st FUSEE

85. see FUZZ   86. see GAUZE   87. see GHAZAL   88. see GAZE
89. see 2nd HAZE   90. see JAZZ   91. see LOZENGE   92. see MATZO
93. see MIZZEN 94. see PIEZO- 95. see 2nd RAZE 96. see SARSAPARILLA
97. see 1st SIZE   98. see 1st and 2nd SIZE   99. see 1st and 2nd SIZE
100. see VIZIER   101. see ZHO   102. see ZINC   103. see ZINC
104. see ZINC   105. see ZIP   106. see ZOEA   107. see ZOEA
108. see ZOISM   109 see ZONE   110. see ZONE   111. see ZONE
112. see ZOEA   113. see ZOO-   114. see ZUPA   115. see ZYGO-
116. see ZYGO-   117. see ZYME

Some Seven-letter Word Lists

This section contains 50 lists of seven-letter words. Each list is headed by a group of six common letters (for example, AENRST, AGINST, DEINRS and EGILNS). Beneath each heading and in order are the 26 letters of the alphabet. If any of the 26 letters plus the six-letter heading can be rearranged to form a seven-letter word, then this will be shown. If more than one seven-letter word can be made, all of them will be shown. For example, on the AENRST list, it can be seen that AENRST plus an A does not make a seven-letter word, so none is shown next to the A on that list; but AENRST plus the letter B makes BANTERS, and this is shown next to the B on that list; better still, AENRST plus the letter C makes several seven-letter words, and these are all shown next to the C on the list. And so on through the alphabet.

You will find it instructive to browse through these lists, learning which letters do and don't go with the various six-letter groups. If you are holding AEILNR and then pick a D as your seventh tile, you may be convinced that you have a word, and, like countless other players before you, you may waste a great deal of time trying to find it. Once you have become familiar with these lists, though, you will know instantly that ADEILNR doesn't form an allowable Scrabble word. (IRELAND, of course, is a proper name, and it isn't in the dictionary, anyway.) You can then begin to decide which letters to play or return to the pool of unused letters.

Though there are 50 lists here, many others could have been produced. Enthusiastic readers might like to compile their own lists. Some six-letter groups that are likely to be worth investigating are these: ADEILR, ADEILT, ADEINR, ADEIRT, ADENRT, AEELRT, AEELST, AEGINT, DEINST, EEINRS, EEINRT and EEINST.

ACGINR

A
B BRACING
C
D CARDING
E
F FARCING
G GRACING
H ARCHING, CHAGRIN,
   CHARING
I
J
K ARCKING (see ARC),
   CARKING, CRAKING,
   RACKING
L
M
N CRANING
O ORGANIC
P CARPING, CRAPING
Q
R
S ARCINGS, RACINGS,
   SACRING, SCARING
T CARTING, CRATING,
   TRACING
U
V CARVING, CRAVING
W
X
Y
Z CRAZING

ADEILS

A
B DISABLE
C SCAILED
D DAIDLES, LADDIES
E AEDILES, DEISEAL
F DISLEAF
G SILAGED
H HALIDES
I DAILIES, LIAISED (see
   LIAISON), SEDILIA
J
K SKAILED
L DALLIES, SALLIED
M MISDEAL, MISLEAD
N DENIALS, SNAILED
O DEASOIL
P ALIPEDS, PAIDLES, PALSIED
Q
R DERAILS, SIDERAL
S AIDLESS, DEASILS
T DETAILS, DILATES
U AUDILES, DEASIUL
V DEVISAL
W
X
Y DIALYSE
Z

A NAIADES
B BANDIES
C CANDIES
D DANDIES
E ANISEED
F
G AGNISED
H
I
J
K KANDIES
L DENIALS, SNAILED
M DEMAINS, MAIDENS,
   MEDIANS
N
O ADONISE, ANODISE,
   SODAINE
P PANSIED (see PANSY),
   SPAINED
Q
R RANDIES, SANDIER, SARDINE
S
T DETAINS, INSTEAD, SAINTED,
   SATINED, STAINED
U
V INVADES
W DEWANIS
X
Y
Z

A
B BRAISED, DARBIES
C RADICES (see RADIX),
   SIDECAR (see 1st SIDE)
D
E DEARIES (see DEAR), READIES
F FRAISED
G AGRISED
H SHADIER
I DAIRIES, DIARIES, DIARISE
   (see DIARY)
J
K DAIKERS, DARKIES (see
   DARK)
L DERAILS, SIDERAL
M MISREAD
N RANDIES, SANDIER, SARDINE
O SOREDIA
P DESPAIR, DIAPERS, PRAISED
Q
R ARRIDES, RAIDERS
S
T ARIDEST, ASTERID (see
   ASTER), ASTRIDE, DISRATE,
   STAIRED, TIRADES
U RESIDUA (see RESIDUE)
V ADVISER, VARDIES
W
X
Y
Z

132

ADEIST

A
B
C DACITES
D
E IDEATES
F DAFTIES (see DAFT), FADIEST (see 1st FADE)
G AGISTED
H
I
J
K
L DETAILS, DILATES
M MISDATE
N DETAINS, INSTEAD, SAINTED, SATINED, STAINED
O IODATES, TOADIES
P
Q
R ARIDEST, ASTERID (see ASTER), ASTRIDE, DISRATE, STAIRED, TIRADES
S DISSEAT, SAIDEST (see 1st SAY)
T
U DAUTIES (see DAUT)
V DATIVES, VISTAED
W DAWTIES (see DAUT), WAISTED
X
Y
Z

ADENRS

A
B
C DANCERS
D DANDERS
E DEANERS, ENDEARS
F FARDENS
G DANGERS, GANDERS, GARDENS
H HANDERS, HARDENS
I RANDIES, SANDIER, SARDINE
J
K DARKENS
L DARNELS, LANDERS (see 1st LAND), SLANDER, SNARLED
M RANDEMS, REMANDS
N
O
P PANDERS
Q
R DARNERS, ERRANDS
S SANDERS, SARSDEN (see SARSEN)
T STANDER
U ASUNDER, DAUNERS
V
W DAWNERS, WANDERS, WARDENS
X
Y
Z ZANDERS

A	AERATES
B	BEATERS, BERATES, REBATES
C	CERATES, CREATES, SECRETA (see SECRET)
D	DEAREST, DERATES, ESTRADE, REASTED
E	
F	AFREETS, FEASTER
G	ERGATES
H	HEATERS, REHEATS
I	SERIATE
J	
K	RETAKES, SAKERET (see SAKER)
L	ELATERS, REALEST, RELATES, STEALER
M	STEAMER, TEAMERS
N	EARNEST, EASTERN, NEAREST
O	ROSEATE
P	REPEATS
Q	
R	SERRATE, TEARERS
S	RESEATS, SAETERS, SEAREST, TEASERS, TESSERA
T	ESTREAT, RESTATE
U	AUSTERE
V	
W	SWEATER
X	
Y	
Z	

A	
B	
C	ANGELIC, ANGLICE (see 3rd ANGLE)
D	ALIGNED, DEALING, LEADING
E	LINEAGE
F	FINAGLE, LEAFING
G	GEALING
H	HEALING
I	
J	
K	LEAKING, LINKAGE
L	
M	MEALING
N	ANELING, EANLING (see EAN), LEANING, NEALING
O	
P	LEAPING, PEALING
Q	
R	LEARING, NARGILE, REALIGN, REGINAL
S	LEASING, LINAGES, SEALING
T	ATINGLE, ELATING, GELATIN, GENITAL
U	
V	LEAVING
W	
X	
Y	
Z	

AEGINR

A
B BEARING
C
D AREDING (see AREAD),
   GRADINE (see GRADE),
   GRAINED, READING
E
F FEARING
G GEARING
H HEARING
I
J
K
L LEARING, NARGILE,
   REALIGN, REGINAL
M MANGIER, REAMING
N EARNING, ENGRAIN,
   GRANNIE, NEARING
O ORIGANE (see ORIGANUM)
P REAPING
Q
R EARRING, GRAINER,
   REARING
S EARINGS (see 3rd EAR),
   ERASING, GAINERS,
   REGAINS, REGINAS,
   SEARING, SERINGA
T GRANITE, INGRATE,
   TEARING
U
V REAVING, VINEGAR
W WEARING
X
Y
Z

AEGINS

A
B
C CEASING
D AGNISED
E
F
G AGEINGS
H
I
J
K SINKAGE
L LEASING, LINAGES, SEALING
M ENIGMAS, GAMINES,
   MEASING, SEAMING
N SEANING
O AGONIES, AGONISE
P SPINAGE (see SPINACH)
Q
R EARINGS (see 3rd EAR),
   ERASING, GAINERS,
   REGAINS, REGINAS,
   SEARING, SERINGA
S
T EASTING, EATINGS, GAINEST,
   INGATES, INGESTA, SEATING,
   TANGIES, TEASING, TSIGANE
   (see TZIGANY)
U GUINEAS
V
W
X
Y
Z

AEGLNS

A ALNAGES, ANLAGES,
   GALENAS, LAGENAS,
   LASAGNE
B BANGLES
C GLANCES
D DANGLES, SLANGED
E
F FLANGES
G LAGGENS
H
I LEASING, LINAGES, SEALING
J JANGLES
K
L LEGLANS (see LEGLIN)
M MANGELS (see MANGEL-
   WURZEL), MANGLES
N
O
P SPANGLE
Q
R ANGLERS
S GLASSEN (see GLASS)
T TANGLES
U ANGELUS, LAGUNES
V
W WANGLES
X
Y
Z

AEILNR

A
B
C CARLINE
D
E
F
G LEARING, NARGILE,
   REALIGN, REGINAL
H HERNIAL, INHALER
I
J
K LANKIER
L RALLINE (see RALLUS)
M MARLINE, MINERAL,
   RAILMEN
N
O AILERON, ALERION,
   ALIENOR
P PEARLIN (see 2nd PEARL),
   PLAINER, PRALINE
Q
R
S NAILERS
T ENTRAIL (see ENTRAILS),
   LATRINE, RATLINE,
   RELIANT, RETINAL, TRENAIL
U
V RAVELIN
W
X
Y INLAYER, NAILERY
Z

A AERIALS
B BAILERS
C CLARIES, SCALIER
D DERAILS, SIDERAL
E REALISE
F
G
H SHALIER (see SHALE)
I SAILIER (see 1st SAIL)
J JAILERS
K SERKALI
L RALLIES
M MAILERS, REALISM
N NAILERS
O
P PARLIES (see PARLIAMENT)
Q
R RAILERS, RERAILS
S AIRLESS (see AIR), SAILERS,
   SERAILS, SERIALS
T REALIST, RETAILS, SALTIER,
   SALTIRE, SLATIER
U
V REVISAL
W WAILERS
X
Y
Z

A
B TRIABLE
C ARTICLE, RECITAL
D DILATER, TRAILED
E ATELIER
F
G
H
I
J
K
L LITERAL
M LAMITER (see LAMETER),
   MALTIER
N ENTRAIL (see ENTRAILS),
   LATRINE, RATLINE,
   RELIANT, RETINAL, TRENAIL
O
P PLAITER
Q
R RETIRAL, RETRIAL, TRAILER
S REALIST, RETAILS, SALTIER,
   SALTIRE, SLATIER
T TERTIAL
U URALITE
V
W
X
Y REALITY (see 1st REAL)
Z

137

AEILST

A
B ALBITES, BESTIAL, LIBATES
  (see LIBATION), STABILE
C ELASTIC, LACIEST, SALICET
  (see SALICACEAE)
D DETAILS, DILATES
E
F
G AIGLETS, LIGATES (see
  LIGAMENT), TAIGLES
H HALITES
I LAITIES
J
K LAKIEST (see 1st and 2nd LAKE),
  TALKIES
L TALLIES
M
N EASTLIN (see EAST), ELASTIN,
  ENTAILS, SALIENT, STANIEL,
  TENAILS
O ISOLATE
P PALIEST (see 1st PALE),
  TALIPES
Q
R REALIST, RETAILS, SALTIER,
  SALTIRE, SLATIER
S
T
U
V
W
X
Y TAILYES
Z LAZIEST

AEINRS

A
B
C ARSENIC, CARNIES, CERASIN
D RANDIES, SANDIER, SARDINE
E
F
G EARINGS (see 3rd EAR),
  ERASING, GAINERS,
  REGAINS, REGINAS,
  SEARING, SERINGA
H ARSHINE, HERNIAS
I
J
K SNAKIER (see SNAKE)
L NAILERS
M MARINES, REMAINS,
  SEMINAR, SIRNAME
N INSNARE
O ERASION
P RAPINES
Q
R SIERRAN
S ARSINES (see ARSENIC)
T NASTIER, RATINES, RESIANT,
  RETAINS, RETINAS, RETSINA,
  STAINER, STARNIE (see
  STERN), STEARIN
U
V RAVINES
W
X
Y
Z

AEINRT

A
B ATEBRIN
C CERTAIN
D DETRAIN, TRAINED
E RETINAE, TRAINEE
F FAINTER
G GRANITE, INGRATE,
  TEARING
H INEARTH
I INERTIA
J
K KERATIN
L ENTRAIL (see ENTRAILS),
  LATRINE, RATLINE,
  RELIANT, RETINAL, TRENAIL
M MINARET, RAIMENT
N ENTRAIN
O OTARINE
P PAINTER, PERTAIN, REPAINT
Q
R TERRAIN, TRAINER
S NASTIER, RATINES, RESIANT,
  RETAINS, RETINAS, RETSINA,
  STAINER, STARNIE (see
  STERN), STEARIN
T INTREAT, ITERANT,
  NATTIER, NITRATE, TERTIAN
U RUINATE, TAURINE,
  URANITE, URINATE
V
W TAWNIER, TINWARE (see TIN)
X
Y
Z

AEINST

A
B BESAINT, BESTAIN
C CANIEST (see CANE), CINEAST
D DETAINS, INSTEAD, SAINTED,
  SATINED, STAINED
E ETESIAN
F FAINEST
G EASTING, EATINGS, GAINEST,
  INGATES, INGESTA, SEATING,
  TANGIES, TEASING, TSIGANE
  (see TZIGANY)
H
I ISATINE
J JANTIES (see JONTY)
K INTAKES
L EASTLIN (see EAST), ELASTIN,
  ENTAILS, SALIENT, STANIEL,
  TENAILS
M INMATES, MANTIES (see
  MANTUA), TAMINES
N
O ATONIES
P PANTIES (see PANTS),
  SPINATE (see SPINE)
Q
R NASTIER, RATINES, RESIANT,
  RETAINS, RETINAS, RETSINA,
  STAINER, STARNIE (see
  STERN), STEARIN
S ENTASIS, SESTINA, TANSIES,
  TISANES
T INSTATE, SATINET
U AUNTIES, SINUATE (see SINUS)
V NAIVEST, VAINEST
W TAWNIES, WANTIES (see
  WANTY)
X
Y
Z ZANIEST

139

A ASTERIA (see ASTER),
  ATRESIA
B BARITES
C RACIEST, STEARIC (see
  STEAR-)
D ARIDEST, ASTERID (see
  ASTER), ASTRIDE, DISRATE,
  STAIRED, TIRADES
E SERIATE
F FAIREST
G AGISTER (see AGIST),
  GAITERS, SEAGIRT, STAGIER
  (see STAGE), STRIGAE,
  TRIAGES
H HASTIER, SHERIAT
I AIRIEST (see AIR), IRISATE (see
  IRIS)
J
K ARKITES, KARITES
L REALIST, RETAILS, SALTIER,
  SALTIRE, SLATIER
M MISRATE
N NASTIER, RATINES, RESIANT,
  RETAINS, RETINAS, RETSINA,
  STAINER, STARNIE (see
  STERN), STEARIN
O OTARIES
P PARTIES, PASTIER, PIASTRE,
  PIRATES, TRAIPSE
Q
R TARRIES, TARSIER
S SATIRES, TIRASSE
T ARTIEST (see ART), ARTISTE,
  ATTIRES, STRIATE, TASTIER,
  TERTIAS
U
V TAIVERS, VASTIER (see VAST)
W WAISTER, WAITERS,
  WARIEST
X
Y
Z

A ARSENAL
B BRANLES, BRANSLE
C LANCERS, RANCELS
D DARNELS, LANDERS,
  SLANDER, SNARLED
E
F SALFERN
G ANGLERS
H
I NAILERS
J
K RANKLES
L
M
N ENSNARL, LANNERS
O ORLEANS
P PLANERS (see 3rd PLANE)
Q
R SNARLER
S RANSELS
T ANTLERS, RENTALS,
  SALTERN, STERNAL
U
V
W
X
Y
Z RANZELS

AELNRT

A
B BRANTLE
C CENTRAL
D
E ALTERNE, ENTERAL (see
ENTERO-), ETERNAL
F
G TANGLER, TRANGLE
H ENTHRAL
I ENTRAIL (see ENTRAILS),
LATRINE, RATLINE,
RELIANT, RETINAL, TRENAIL
J
K
L
M
N LANTERN
O
P PLANTER, REPLANT
Q
R
S ANTLERS, RENTALS,
SALTERN, STERNAL
T TRENTAL
U NEUTRAL
V VENTRAL
W
X
Y
Z

AELNST

A SEALANT (see 1st SEAL)
B
C CANTLES, LANCETS
D DENTALS, SLANTED
E ELANETS, LEANEST
F
G TANGLES
H HANTLES
I EASTLIN (see EAST), ELASTIN,
ENTAILS, SALIENT, STANIEL,
TENAILS
J
K LANKEST
L
M LAMENTS, MANTELS,
MANTLES
N STANNEL
O ETALONS
P PLANETS, PLATENS
Q
R ANTLERS, RENTALS,
SALTERN, STERNAL
S
T LATTENS, TALENTS
U ELUANTS
V LEVANTS
W
X
Y STANYEL (see STANIEL)
Z ZELANTS (see ZEAL)

A

B ALBERTS, BLASTER, LABRETS
   (see LABRUM), STABLER

C CLARETS, SCARLET,
   TARCELS

D DARTLES (see 1st DART)

E ELATERS, REALEST,
   RELATES, STEALER

F FALTERS

G LARGEST

H HALTERS, HARSLET,
   LATHERS, SLATHER,
   THALERS

I REALIST, RETAILS, SALTIER,
   SALTIRE, SLATIER

J

K STALKER, TALKERS

L STELLAR, TELLARS

M ARMLETS (see ARM),
   MARTELS

N ANTLERS, RENTALS,
   SALTERN, STERNAL

O OESTRAL (see OESTRUS)

P PLASTER, PLATERS, STAPLER

Q

R

S ARTLESS (see ART), LASTERS
   (see 1st and 2nd LAST), SALTERS
   (see SALT), SLATERS, TARSELS

T RATTLES, SLATTER (see
   SLATTERN), TATLERS

U SALUTER

V TRAVELS, VARLETS

W WASTREL (see WASTE)

X

Y

Z

A

B BANTERS

C CANTERS, CARNETS,
   NECTARS, RECANTS,
   TANRECS, TRANCES

D STANDER

E EARNEST, EASTERN,
   NEAREST

F

G ARGENTS, GARNETS,
   STRANGE

H ANTHERS, HARTENS,
   THENARS

I NASTIER, RATINES, RESIANT,
   RETAINS, RETINAS, RETSINA,
   STAINER, STARNIE (see
   STERN), STEARIN

J

K RANKEST, STARKEN (see
   STARK), TANKERS

L ANTLERS, RENTALS,
   SALTERN, STERNAL

M MARTENS, SARMENT,
   SMARTEN

N TANNERS

O ATONERS, SENATOR,
   TREASON

P ARPENTS, ENTRAPS,
   PARENTS, PASTERN,
   TREPANS

Q

R ERRANTS (see ERR), RANTERS

S SARSNET, TRANSES

T NATTERS, RATTENS

U AUNTERS, NATURES,
   SAUNTER

V SERVANT, TAVERNS,
   VERSANT

W WANTERS (see 1st WANT)

X

Y

Z

142

AEORST

A
B BOASTER, BOATERS,
   BORATES
C COASTER
D DOATERS (see DOTE),
   ROASTED, TORSADE (see
   TORSE)
E ROSEATE
F
G ORGEATS, STORAGE (see
   STORE)
H EARSHOT (see EAR)
I OTARIES
J
K
L OESTRAL (see OESTRUS)
M AMORETS
N ATONERS, SENATOR,
   TREASON
O
P ESPARTO, SEAPORT (see SEA)
Q
R ROASTER
S
T ROTATES, TOASTER
U
V
W
X
Y
Z

AGHINS

A
B BASHING
C ACHINGS, CASHING,
   CHASING
D DASHING, SHADING
E
F FASHING
G GASHING
H HASHING
I
J
K SHAKING
L HALSING, LASHING
M MASHING, SHAMING
N
O
P HASPING, PHASING,
   SHAPING
Q
R GARNISH, SHARING
S SASHING
T HASTING, TASHING
U ANGUISH
V HAVINGS, SHAVING
W SHAWING, WASHING
X
Y HAYINGS (see 1st HAY)
Z HAZINGS (see 2nd HAZE)

A
B
C CARTING, CRATING,
  TRACING
D DARTING, TRADING
E GRANITE, INGRATE,
  TEARING
F FARTING, RAFTING
G GRATING, TARGING
H
I RAITING (see RET)
J
K KARTING
L RATLING
M
N RANTING
O ORATING
P PARTING, PRATING,
  TRAPING (see TRAIPSE)
Q
R TARRING
S RATINGS, STARING
T RATTING
U
V
W
X
Y GIANTRY (see GIANT)
Z

A AGAINST
B BASTING
C ACTINGS (see ACT), CASTING
D
E EASTING, EATINGS, GAINEST,
  INGATES, INGESTA, SEATING,
  TANGIES, TEASING, TSIGANE
  (see TZIGANY)
F FASTING
G GATINGS (see 1st GATE),
  STAGING
H HASTING, TASHING
I
J
K SKATING, STAKING,
  TAKINGS
L ANGLIST (see 3rd ANGLE),
  LASTING, SALTING, SLATING,
  STALING (see 1st, 3rd and 5th
  STALE)
M MASTING, TAMINGS (see
  TAME)
N ANTINGS (see ANT), STANING
O AGONIST
P PASTING
Q
R RATINGS, STARING
S
T STATING, TASTING
U SAUTING
V STAVING
W TAWINGS (see 2nd TAW),
  WASTING
X TAXINGS (see TAX)
Y STAYING
Z

DEENRS

A DEANERS, ENDEARS
B BENDERS
C
D REDDENS
E NEEDERS, SERENED (see 1st
  SERENE), SNEERED
F FENDERS
G GENDERS
H
I DENIERS, NEREIDS, RESINED
J
K
L LENDERS, SLENDER
M MENDERS
N
O ENDORSE
P SPENDER
Q
R RENDERS
S REDNESS, SENDERS
T STERNED, TENDERS
U ENDURES, ENSURED
V VENDERS
W
X
Y
Z DZERENS

DEINRS

A RANDIES, SANDIER, SARDINE
B BINDERS, REBINDS
C CINDERS, DISCERN, RESCIND
D
E DENIERS, NEREIDS, RESINED
F FINDERS, FRIENDS
G DINGERS (see 1st DING),
  ENGIRDS
H HINDERS
I INSIDER
J
K REDSKIN
L
M MINDERS, REMINDS
N DINNERS
O DONSIER, INDORSE,
  ROSINED, SORDINE (see
  SORDO)
P PINDERS
Q
R
S
T TINDERS
U INSURED
V
W REWINDS, WINDERS
X
Y
Z

DEIRST

A ARIDEST, ASTERID (see ASTER), ASTRIDE, DISRATE, STAIRED, TIRADES
B BESTRID (see BESTRIDE)
C CREDITS, DIRECTS
D
E REISTED
F
G
H DITHERS, SHIRTED
I DIRTIES
J
K
L
M
N TINDERS
O EDITORS, ROISTED (see ROISTER), ROSITED (see ROSET), SORTIED (see SORTIE), STEROID, STORIED (see STOREY and STORY), TRIODES
P SPIRTED, STRIPED
Q
R STIRRED
S STRIDES
T
U DUSTIER, REDUITS, STUDIER
V DIVERTS, STRIVED
W
X
Y
Z

EEIRST

A SERIATE
B REBITES
C RECITES
D REISTED
E EERIEST
F
G
H HEISTER
I
J
K
L LEISTER, STERILE
M METIERS, TREMIES
N ENTIRES, ENTRIES, NERITES (see NERITA), TRENISE
O
P RESPITE
Q
R ETRIERS, REITERS, RESTIER (see RESTY), RETIRES, RETRIES, TERRIES
S
T TESTIER
U
V RESTIVE
W
X
Y
Z

147

EENRST

A   EARNEST, EASTERN, NEAREST
B
C   CENTRES, TENRECS
D   STERNED, TENDERS
E   ENTREES, RETENES
F
G   GERENTS, REGENTS
H
I   ENTIRES, ENTRIES, NERITES (see NERITA), TRENISE
J
K
L   RELENTS
M
N   RENNETS, TENNERS (see TEN)
O
P   PRESENT, REPENTS, SERPENT
Q
R   RENTERS, STERNER
S   RESENTS
T   TENTERS (see 1st and 4th TENT), TESTERN
U   NEUTERS, TENURES, TUREENS
V   VENTERS, VENTRES
W   WESTERN
X   EXTERNS (see EXTERNAL)
Y   STYRENE, YESTERN (see YESTER)
Z

EGILNS

A   LEASING, LINAGES, SEALING
B   BINGLES
C
D   DINGLES, ELDINGS, SINGLED
E   SEELING (see 1st SEEL)
F   SELFING (see SELF)
G   GINGLES, NIGGLES, SNIGGLE (see SNIG)
H   SHINGLE
I   SEILING
J   JINGLES
K   KINGLES
L   LEGLINS, LINGELS, LINGLES, SELLING
M   MINGLES
N
O   ELOIGNS, LEGIONS
P   PINGLES, SPIGNEL
Q
R   GIRNELS, LINGERS, SLINGER
S   SINGLES
T   GLISTEN, SINGLET, TINGLES
U   LUNGIES
V
W   SLEWING, SWINGLE
X
Y
Z   ZINGELS

EGILNT

A ATINGLE, ELATING, GELATIN, GENITAL
B BELTING
C
D GLINTED, TINGLED
E GENTILE
F FELTING
G
H ENLIGHT, LIGHTEN
I LIGNITE (see 1st LIGNUM)
J JINGLET (see JINGLE)
K KINGLET (see KING)
L TELLING
M MELTING
N
O LENTIGO
P PELTING
Q
R RINGLET, TINGLER, TRINGLE
S GLISTEN, SINGLET, TINGLES
T ETTLING, LETTING
U ELUTING (see ELUTION)
V
W WELTING, WINGLET (see 1st WING)
X
Y
Z

EGINRS

A EARINGS (see 3rd EAR), ERASING, GAINERS, REGAINS, REGINAS, SEARING, SERINGA
B
C CRINGES
D DINGERS (see 1st DING), ENGIRDS
E GREISEN
F FINGERS, FRINGES
G GINGERS, NIGGERS, SNIGGER
H
I
J
K
L GIRNELS, LINGERS, SLINGER
M
N ENRINGS, GINNERS (see 2nd GIN)
O ERINGOS, IGNORES, REGIONS, SIGNORE (see SIGNOR)
P SPRINGE
Q
R ERRINGS, RINGERS, SERRING (see SERRIED)
S INGRESS, RESIGNS, SIGNERS, SINGERS
T RESTING, STINGER
U REUSING, RUEINGS (see 2nd RUE)
V SERVING, VERSING
W SWINGER, WINGERS (see 1st WING)
X
Y SYRINGE
Z

EGINRT

A GRANITE, INGRATE,
  TEARING
B
C
D
E INTEGER, TEERING, TREEING
F
G
H RIGHTEN
I IGNITER, TIERING (see TIER),
  TIGRINE (see TIGER)
J
K
L RINGLET, TINGLER, TRINGLE
M
N RENTING, RINGENT,
  TERNING (see TERNE)
O GENITOR
P
Q
R
S RESTING, STINGER
T GITTERN, RETTING
U TRUEING
V VERTING (see 2nd VERT)
W TREWING
X
Y
Z

EGINST

A EASTING, EATINGS, INGATES,
  INGESTA, SEATING, TANGIES,
  TEASING, TSIGANE (see
  TZIGANY)
B BESTING
C
D NIDGETS, STINGED
E
F
G
H NIGHEST
I IGNITES
J JESTING
K
L GLISTEN, SINGLET, TINGLES
M TEMSING
N NESTING
O
P
Q
R RESTING, STINGER
S INGESTS, SIGNETS
T SETTING, TESTING
U GUNITES
V VESTING
W STEWING, TWINGES,
  WESTING
X
Y
Z

EHIRST

A HASTIER, SHERIAT
B HERBIST
C CITHERS, RICHEST
D DITHERS, SHIRTED
E HEISTER
F SHIFTER
G SIGHTER (see 1st SIGHT)
H HITHERS
I
J
K
L SLITHER
M HERMITS
N
O HERIOTS
P HIPSTER
Q
R
S
T HITTERS
U HIRSUTE
V THRIVES
W WITHERS, WRITHES
X
Y
Z ZITHERS

EILNST

A EASTLIN (see EAST), ELASTIN,
   ENTAILS, SALIENT, STANIEL,
   TENAILS
B
C CLIENTS, STENCIL
D DENTILS (see 2nd DENT)
E TENSILE
F
G GLISTEN, SINGLET, TINGLES
H
I
J
K LENTISK, TINKLES
L LENTILS, LINTELS
M
N LINNETS
O ENTOILS, LIONETS
P PINTLES
Q
R LINTERS, SNIRTLE (see SNIRT)
S ENLISTS, LISTENS, TINSELS
T
U LUTEINS, UNTILES, UTENSIL
V
W WESTLIN (see WEST)
X
Y
Z

EILRST

A REALIST, RETAILS, SALTIER, SALTIRE, SLATIER
B BLISTER
C
D
E LEISTER, STERILE
F FILTERS, LIFTERS, TRIFLES
G GLISTER, GRISTLE
H SLITHER
I SILTIER
J
K KIRTLES
L RILLETS (see RILL), STILLER, TILLERS, TRELLIS
M
N LINTERS, SNIRTLE (see SNIRT)
O LOITERS, TOILERS
P SPIRTLE, TRIPLES
Q
R
S
T LITTERS, SLITTER (see SLIT), STILTER (see STILT), TESTRIL, TILTERS (see 2nd TILT), TITLERS (see TITLE)
U LUSTIER, RULIEST (see RULE), RUTILES
V
W
X
Y
Z

EINRST

A NASTIER, RATINES, RESIANT, RETAINS, RETINAS, RETSINA, STAINER, STARNIE (see STERN), STEARIN
B
C CRETINS
D TINDERS
E ENTIRES, ENTRIES, NERITES (see NERITA), TRENISE
F SNIFTER (see SNIFF)
G RESTING, STINGER
H
I
J
K STINKER, TINKERS
L LINTERS, SNIRTLE (see SNIRT)
M MINSTER, MINTERS (see 1st MINT)
N INTERNS, TINNERS (see TIN)
O NORITES, ORIENTS, STONIER (see STONE), TERSION (see TERSE), TRIONES
P NIPTERS, PTERINS
Q
R
S INSERTS, SINTERS
T STINTER (see 1st STINT), TINTERS
U TRIUNES, UNITERS (see UNITE)
V INVERTS, STRIVEN
W TWINERS (see 1st TWINE), WINTERS
X
Y SINTERY (see SINTER)
Z

EIORST

A OTARIES
B ORBIEST (see 1st ORB)
C EROTICS, TERCIOS
D EDITORS, ROISTED (see ROISTER), ROSITED (see ROSET), SORTIED (see SORTIE), STEROID, STORIED (see STOREY and STORY), TRIODES
E
F FOISTER, FORTIES
G GOITRES, GORIEST
H HERIOTS
I RIOTISE (see RIOT)
J
K ROKIEST (see ROKE)
L LOITERS, TOILERS
M EROTISM, MOISTER
N NORITES, ORIENTS, STONIER (see STONE), TERSION (see TERSE), TRIONES
O ROOTIES (see ROOTY), SOOTIER, TOORIES
P PERIOST (see PERIOSTEUM), REPOSIT, RIPOSTE, ROPIEST (see ROPE)
Q
R RIOTERS, ROISTER
S ROSIEST, SORITES, SORTIES, STORIES
T STOITER (see STOIT)
U
V TORSIVE (see TORSION)
W
X
Y
Z

ELORST

A OESTRAL (see OESTRUS)
B BOLSTER, BOLTERS, LOBSTER
C COLTERS, COSTREL, LECTORS
D OLDSTER (see OLD), STRODLE
E
F FLORETS (see FLORA)
G
H HOLSTER, HOSTLER
I LOITERS, TOILERS
J JOLTERS
K
L TOLLERS (see 2nd TOLL)
M
N LENTORS
O ROOTLES (see 2nd ROOT)
P PETROLS
Q
R
S OSTLERS, STEROLS, TORSELS
T TOLTERS
U ELUTORS (see ELUTION), OUTLERS
V REVOLTS
W TROWELS
X
Y
Z

153

A ATONERS, SENATOR,
   TREASON
B SORBENT (see 3rd SORB)
C CORNETS
D RODENTS, SNORTED
E
F
G
H HORNETS, SHORTEN,
   THRONES
I NORITES, ORIENTS, STONIER
   (see STONE), TERSION (see
   TERSE), TRIONES
J
K STONKER
L LENTORS, LORNEST
M MENTORS, MONSTER
N STONERN (see STONE)
O ENROOTS
P POSTERN
Q
R SNORTER
S STONERS, TENSORS (see
   TENSE)
T ROTTENS, SNOTTER,
   STENTOR (see 2nd STENT)
U TENOURS (see TENOR),
   TONSURE
V
W
X
Y TYRONES (see TIRO)
Z

A AUNTERS, NATURES,
   SAUNTER
B BRUNETS, BUNTERS,
   BURNETS, BURSTEN (see
   BURST)
C ENCRUST
D RETUNDS
E NEUTERS, TENURES,
   TUREENS
F
G GUNTERS, GURNETS (see
   GURNARD), SURGENT (see 2nd
   SURGE)
H HUNTERS, SHUNTER
I TRIUNES, UNITERS (see
   UNITE)
J
K
L RUNLETS
M STERNUM
N RUNNETS, STUNNER
O TENOURS (see TENOR),
   TONSURE
P PUNSTER, PUNTERS (see 1st
   and 2nd PUNT)
Q
R RETURNS, TURNERS
S UNRESTS
T ENTRUST, NUTTERS (see NUT)
U
V
W
X
Y
Z

EORSTU

A
B
C SCOUTER
D DETOURS, DOUREST,
   DOUTERS (see DOUT),
   OUTREDS, ROUSTED
E
F
G
H SOUTHER (see SOUTH)
I TOUSIER (see TOUSE)
J
K
L ELUTORS (see ELUTION),
   OUTLERS
M
N TENOURS (see TENOR),
   TONSURE
O
P PETROUS, POSTURE,
   POUTERS, SEPTUOR,
   SPOUTER, TROUPES
Q QUESTOR, QUOTERS,
   ROQUETS, TORQUES
R RETOURS, ROUSTER,
   ROUTERS (see 3rd ROUT),
   TOURERS
S OUSTERS, SOUTERS
T STOUTER, TOUTERS
U
V
W
X
Y
Z

GINOST

A AGONIST
B
C COSTING, GNOSTIC
D DOTINGS
E
F
G
H HOSTING
I
J
K STOKING
L LINGOTS
M
N STONING
O SOOTING
P POSTING, STOPING
Q
R ROSTING, SORTING,
   STORING, TRIGONS
S STINGOS, TOSSING
T SOTTING
U OUSTING, OUTINGS,
   TOUSING
V STOVING
W STOWING, TOWINGS (see 1st
   TOW), TOWSING
X
Y TOYINGS (see TOY)
Z

155

100 Strange Words

Frequently, a Scrabble player will inform his opponent that his rack contains such awful letters that he cannot make any word at all. Often true, but often an exaggeration. This list is a haphazard selection of 100 weird words from *Chambers Twentieth Century Dictionary* (with 1977 Supplement). Surprisingly, none is shown by the dictionary as being foreign or obsolete. All the words are allowable under the rules of the National Scrabble Championship from 1980 onwards.

You may never get an opportunity to play any of these words, and even if you could play just one of them, it might not be your best move, anyway. Even so, to be aware that such outlandish-looking words do exist and could be used if necessary may be some consolation to you at some time. Even the most abysmal set of letters on your rack *might* contain some esoteric but allowable word.

ADUNC	ELCHI	KGOTLA	OGDOAD
APNOEA	ELEVON	KLEPHT	OLLAV
ASPHYXY	EUOI	KRIS	OMMATEA
AUTOVAC	EUTEXIA	KWELA	OONT
BAETYL	FASTI	LLANO	OUSTITI
BHISTY	FRAKTUR	LOGLOG	PASHM
CEDI	GHARRI	MATLO	PASPY
CHARQUI	GHEE	MITZVAH	PFENNIG
CIPPI	GOLEM	MOWA	PHIZOG
CNIDA	GWYNIAD	MPRET	PRUH
CRWTH	HAIKU	MUZHIK	PYGARG
DARG	HUZOOR	MVULE	REBEC
DEEV	HWYL	NABK	RHABDOM
DJIBBAH	IKEBANA	NAEVI	RHIZIC
DOSEH	ILKADAY	NERKA	RYEPECK
DVORNIK	INYALA	NGAIO	RYOT
DWALE	ISSEI	NUNATAK	SADHU
EIRACK	JEZAIL	NYANZA	SCYE

SECCO	THALWEG	UNCI	XERAFIN
SMYTRIE	THYRSI	UPTAK	YACCA
SOFTA	TOPHI	VAKASS	YAKHDAN
SOWFF	TSOTSI	VRIL	YCLEPT
SYBOW	UGLI	WHUMMLE	YLEM
TATOU	ULICON	WINNA	YNAMBU
TAUTOG	UMWHILE	WRAXLE	ZEUXITE

Some Unallowable Words

Throughout this book there are lists of words that the Scrabble player ought to know, two-letter words, three-letter words, words with Js in, seven-letter words, words with vowels, and so on. This section, though, contains a list of 100 words which, as familiar as they may seem, would not be allowed at the National Scrabble Championship for one reason or another.

AARDVARK shown as foreign (South African)

ADZ not listed; shown only as 'adze'

AGGRO shown as an abbreviation

AIRINESS not listed

AITCH a letter

ANTI not listed as a word in its own right; only the prefix 'anti-' is shown

APER not listed

AQUA shown as foreign (Latin)

AR a letter

ARMOR shown as foreign (U.S.)

BACCY shown as an abbreviation

BAGEL shown as foreign (U.S.)

BARNET not listed (it is short for 'barnet fair', hair)

BOMBE shown as foreign (French)

BRONCO shown as foreign (U.S.)

BRUT shown as foreign (French)

CASTANET the plural form 'castanets' is shown, but the singular form isn't

CASTRATO shown as foreign (Italian)

CENTER shown as foreign (American) or Shakespearean

CINE not listed

COLESLAW shown only in its hyphenated form, 'cole-slaw'

DEEJAY shown only in its hyphenated form, 'dee-jay'

DEFENSE shown as foreign (U.S.)

DIETER Shakespearean

DODGEMS shown with an initial capital letter

DUKW shown with all four letters capitalised

DUVET shown as foreign (French)

EF a letter

EME obsolete

EPSILON a letter

ETA a letter

FONDU not listed; shown only as 'fondue'

GAMMA a letter

GATEAUX the -X plural is not listed at 'gâteau', leaving 'gâteaus' to be inferred as the plural form; 'beaux' and 'châteaux' are shown as the only plurals of 'beau' and 'château', while both 'bureaus' and 'bureaux' are shown for 'bureau'

IDEM shown as foreign (Latin)

JAPER not listed

JEHU shown with an initial capital letter

JEW shown with an initial capital letter

KAPPA a letter

MANANA shown as foreign (Spanish)

METHS shown as an abbreviation

MIDI not listed as a word in its own right; only the prefix 'midi-' is shown

MINI shown as an abbreviation

MINIBUS obsolete, but the hyphenated form 'mini-bus' is not obsolete

MISDIET Spenserian

MOANER not listed

MONSIEUR shown with an initial capital letter

MU a letter

MUON shown as an abbreviation

NAN not listed

NEBULAS not listed; the plural form of 'nebula' is shown only as 'nebulae'

NU a letter

NUDGED 'nudge' is shown only as a noun, not a verb

NUDGING 'nudge' is shown only as a noun, not a verb

OMICRON a letter

OS shown as foreign (Latin)

PASTA shown as foreign (Italian)

PERSONA shown as foreign (Latin)

PHI a letter

PHLOX shown with an initial capital letter

PHOTO shown as an abbreviation

PIZZA shown as foreign (Italian)

POMMY shown as foreign (Australian)

POXIER 'poxy' is not listed

POXIEST 'poxy' is not listed

POXY not listed

PSI a letter

QUAKER shown only with an initial capital letter; there is no meaning such as 'one who quakes'

RAH shown as an abbreviation

REX obsolete; also shown with an initial capital letter

RHO a letter

RUMBAED 'rumba' is shown only as a noun, not a verb

RUMBAING 'rumba' is shown only as a noun, not a verb

SEDATED 'sedate' is shown only as an adjective, not a verb

SEDATING 'sedate' is shown only as an adjective, not a verb

SENOR shown with an initial capital letter

SENORA shown with an initial capital letter

SENORITA shown with an initial capital letter

SITCOM shown as an abbreviation (in the 1977 Supplement)

TELE only the prefix 'tele-' is listed

TENSED 'tense' is shown only as an adjective and noun, not a verb

TENSING 'tense' is shown only as an adjective and noun, not a verb

TERRA shown as foreign (Latin and Italian)

TOENAIL shown only in its hyphenated form 'toe-nail'

TRANNIE shown as an abbreviation (in the 1977 Supplement)

TSARINA not listed

UPSILON a letter

VEGAN shown with an initial capital letter

VIN shown as foreign (French)

WOMBY Shakespearean

XI a letter

YID shown with an initial capital letter

YOGURT not listed; only the forms 'yoghourt', 'yoghurt' and 'yaourt' are shown

YPSILON a letter

ZESTED 'zest' is shown only as a noun, not a verb

ZESTING 'zest' is shown only as a noun, not a verb

ZESTY not listed

ZOWIE shown as foreign (U.S.)

ZULU shown with an initial capital letter

6
Scrabble Variations

Different games that can be played on a Scrabble board, from Un-Scrabble right through to solo Scrabble.

There are many variations that can be introduced into the game of Scrabble. House rules can be introduced, certain categories of words which are normally barred may be allowed, certain categories of words which are normally allowed may be barred, extra tiles can be incorporated into the game, time limits can be introduced, words can be totally dispensed with, and the game can be played in foreign languages. A number of the variations are examined here in more detail.

Variation Number 1

Using the official rules, some players impose a limit on the number of times that a player may exchange his letters during the course of a game. For example, at the National Scrabble Championship, the number of exchanges is limited to three. Some players choose two, others four.

Variation Number 2

The use of obsolete words may be barred, even though they may appear in the agreed dictionary. This is one of the variations to the official rules which is introduced at the National Scrabble Championship.

Variation Number 3

Some players impose a time limit for each move that players make. At the National Scrabble Championship, there is a blanket limit of two minutes per move. Some players prefer to be more flexible, while still retaining the idea of a limit. They use chess clocks, where a player is allowed a total amount of time for all his moves, say, 30 minutes, but how he chooses to divide up this time between individual moves is up to him. If he needs only ten seconds to consider a certain move, all well and good. If he has a particularly tricky situation to ponder, he may well feel like using seven or eight minutes of his total allotted time. This is a good idea, the main problem being the accessibility of chess clocks.

Variation Number 4

Some players introduce a very short time limit for each move, say, 15 seconds. In such a 'speeded-up' version of the game, there is very little time to think or plan ahead. It is very much a question of making the first reasonable score that you can see, and then not getting too upset when you realise that you missed a 50-point bonus. A quickie game like this can be used to fill in an odd 15 minutes or so.

Variation Number 5

The rule regarding the use of a dictionary solely to check a word's allowability when it has been challenged may be abandoned. There are two ways in which players are allowed to use the dictionary. In the first one, all players are allowed to make as much use of the dictionary as they wish at any time during the course of the game, looking for words to play. In this game, ideally, each player should have his own copy of the (same) dictionary. A different way of allowing players access to a dictionary is to allow its use only while their opponent is making his move. This method puts the pressure on player number 2 to complete his turn as quickly as possible. After all, the more quickly player 2 goes, the less chance there is of player number 1 finding a useful word in the dictionary. Allowing dictionaries to be used during the game, before words are played, is a good way to enlarge players' vocabularies, especially young players and novices.

Variation Number 6

The official rules state that once a blank has been played, it cannot be moved. This particular variation, though, allows a player to pick up a blank from the board, replacing it with an equivalent tile. For example, if the word UN*ILED was on the board (with the * representing the letter T), then at a later stage, any player may take the blank and put down a real T in its place. A player is not allowed to put down a different letter to what the blank was originally stated to be, even if a new word results. If UN*ILED was on the board, a player is not allowed to pick up the blank, replace it with an F, and make the new word UNFILED, even though that is a word. There are variations on this variation even. One of them allows for such a substitution play to take place *instead* of a player putting letters on the board or exchanging letters; another version allows for a player to make such a substitution play and *then* play or exchange letters. Try both versions, but ensure that all players fully understand the precise rules.

Variation Number 7

If you have access to two Scrabble sets with the same size tiles, put all 200 tiles into one pool. Though there are 225 squares on the board, it is most unlikely that all 200 tiles could be played. Play continues until a player cannot make a move and he has used up the agreed number of exchanges. Again, make sure that all players understand how all the scores are adjusted at the end of the game.

Variation Number 8

The official rules don't allow for the use of proper names, but you might care to try a game or two where these are allowed. You might just choose to allow any proper name shown in your dictionary. If you were playing with *Chambers Twentieth Century Dictionary*, you might want to allow the personal names which appear in a special section at the back of the dictionary. You may want to go even further, allowing any place-names which appear in a chosen atlas or gazetteer. As long as all the players know the rules, there is no limit as to what proper names could be allowed.

Variation Number 9

How about playing thematic Scrabble? All the words played have to have some common theme. For example, if the theme was motoring, words such as CAR, GEAR, CLUTCH, and PISTONS would be quite acceptable. There may be one or two problems, though, in deciding whether a particular word comes within the bounds of the theme or not. This is not such a serious variation, though it may be fun to play with children or after you have had a drink or two!

Variation Number 10

Take a standard Scrabble set and split the tiles into two heaps. Put the consonants in one heap, and the vowels in the other. Treat the Ys as vowels, and put one blank in each heap. You now have two pools. Then play the game normally, allowing players to take their letters from either or both pools as they wish. If a player makes a five-letter word and needs to pick up five new letters, how many he takes from each bag is up to him. He might choose five consonants and no vowels, four and one, three and two, and so on. Though a blank may have come from the vowel pool, it may be used as a vowel or a consonant. The same applies to the blank from the consonant pool.

Variation Number 11

Scrabble can be played through the post. Expensive as the post is, even second-class mail, there are flourishing postal Scrabble clubs. Players make their moves and receive their letters via a referee, or 'games-master'. The games-master plays no other part in the game at all. Of course, players have unlimited use of the dictionary before making their moves. This can also be an excellent way to improve one's Scrabble vocabulary.

Variation Number 12

A player without a face-to-face opponent or any postal opponents, perhaps wanting to while away the odd half hour or so, can immerse himself in any of the several solitaire versions of the game. In one version, all the tiles are placed face down, well-shuffled, and the player selects seven tiles. He attempts to make a word in the normal way, and scores it. Then, he selects from the pool the number of letters necessary, bringing his rack up to its usual complement of seven letters. In this version, he can make openings for himself, just as he would if he was playing in a two-player game. In a second version of solitaire Scrabble, the player attempts to get as high a score possible at every move. After each move, he puts his remaining letters back into the pool, mixes them thoroughly, and takes seven new letters. Though the concept of making openings still applies, the likelihood of 50-point bonuses falls off dramatically. Bonuses can now only be achieved if the player is lucky enough to pull seven letters out of the pool that just happen to make a word. In both these versions of solitaire Scrabble, the player can compare his latest scores with scores from earlier games.

Variation Number 13

Un-Scrabble is a game described in the booklet of official rules that is supplied with each set of the game by J.W. Spear and Son Limited. Un-Scrabble consists of *removing* letters from the board of a completed Scrabble game. It is relatively quick and can be played by any number of players. The winner of the preceding normal Scrabble game begins, and each player follows in turn. Each player removes at least one and not more than six letters from the board, according to the following rules: the tiles removed at each turn must be taken from one word still remaining on the board, though not necessarily from adjacent squares; after each player's turn, all tiles remaining on the board must form complete words which are properly interconnected with all the other words. The game ends when all the tiles have been removed from the board or when it is impossible to continue without breaking the rules. Scores can be kept in two ways. Method 1: the letter tiles may be counted at their face point values as they are removed from the board, and the player who scores the highest total number of points wins. Method 2: tiles are counted at values modified by the premium squares from which they are taken. Double-letter-score and triple-letter-score premium squares apply to the letters which are removed from them; and double-word-score and triple-word-score premium squares apply to the total value of the letters removed at the time that the premium square is uncovered. The winner is the player with the highest total score at the end of the game.

Variation Number 14

One of the strangest variations is this one, where the use of words has been dispensed with. Players concentrate on making high-scoring garbled letter sequences. Players take letters from the pool in the usual way, always having seven at a time on their racks. The tiles are placed on the board in order to give the highest scores possible. All sequences of letters, whether they are words are not, are valid. Scores are calculated in the usual way. The game becomes an exercise in using the premium squares and the high-value letters without being constricted by the need to form words as well! The 50-point bonus is done away with, otherwise players would continually put down seven letters, claiming a bonus at every turn. The concept of challenging disappears, too. Without words, there is nothing left to challenge. All the associated problems about choosing dictionaries, allowing some words in them, but barring others, disappear as well. This variation doesn't turn out to be quite so anarchic as it may sound.

Variation Number 15

Scrabble drives and tournaments are not so much a variation in the way of actually playing the game as an excuse for getting together anything from 10 to 50 people at a time, all playing Scrabble and competing against each other. Every player will get to play the same number of games, usually three or four. The winner of the tournament is the player with the highest total score after all the games have been completed. If required, there can be some kind of bonus system which rewards winning, so that a player scoring 1900 points and winning all four of his games is deemed to have done better than a player scoring 1950 points but who won only three of his four games. Many Scrabble clubs organise such tournaments. There are even inter-club matches, lasting perhaps a whole weekend and involving nine or even a dozen games.

Variation Number 16

Scrabble can be played in foreign languages. Playing in languages other than English is more than just a question of playing with a standard English set and putting down foreign words. Foreign sets include different numbers of letters, different distributions, different point values for some of the tiles, and even different rules. Foreign-language Scrabble sets are available in Great Britain, usually from specialist games shops. Among languages that are currently available are French, German, Spanish, Italian, Dutch, Afrikaans, Russian, and Arabic. Spanish Scrabble contains 100 letters, some of which will seem rather odd to an eye unaccustomed to Spanish. There is one tile marked CH, worth 5 points; there is a tile marked LL, worth 8 points; there is one tile with an N that has a tilde accent over it (Ñ), worth 8 points; and there is an RR tile, worth 8 points. The Q is only worth 5 points, and there is no K at all. Dutch Scrabble has 104 letters, including 18 Es, 10 Ns, 2 Js, and 2 Zs. The J is worth only 4 points, the F 5 points, and the Z 6 points. French Scrabble has no acute or grave accent on any of the Es, but it does have 15 of them. The Q is only worth 8 points, and there are 5 letters (KWXYZ) all worth 10 points. The German set contains a massive 119 tiles. As well as there being As, Os and Us, there is also one A with an umlaut (Ä), an O with an umlaut (Ö), and a U with an umlaut (Ü). There are 16 Es, 10 Ns and 8 Ss. The Z is worth a mere 3 points, the J is worth 6, the K is worth 3, and the Y is worth 10. Which is strange, because there is no letter Y in the German language. Any words known to a German player having a Y will invariably be borrowings from other languages, such as YACHT and YAK. The strangest thing, though, about German Scrabble is that players have *eight* letters at a time on their racks, and they get 50-point bonuses for playing all eight tiles at once! This probably means that German Scrabble players are far more used to seeing words go down covering two triple-word-score squares at a time. To be true to the spirit of the game, perhaps the board size should have been increased to 17 squares by 17 squares for German players.